FIX, FREEZE, FEAST

THE DELICIOUS, MONEY-SAVING WAY TO FEED YOUR FAMILY

KATI NEVILLE & LINDSAY TKACSIK

Storey Publishing

TO OUR HUSBANDS AND CHILDREN.

The mission of Storey Publishing is to serve our customers by publishing practical information that encourages personal independence in harmony with the environment.

Edited by Margaret Sutherland
Art direction by Alethea Morrison
Cover and text design by Ph.D
Text production by Liseann Karandisecky

Illustrations © by Ph.D
Indexed by Chris Lindemer

The information in this book is true and complete to the best of our knowledge. All recommendations are made without guarantee on the part of the author or Storey Publishing. The author and publisher disclaim any liability in connection with the use of this information. For additional information, please contact Storey Publishing, 210 MASS MoCA Way, North Adams, MA 01247.

Storey books are available for special premium and promotional uses and for customized editions. For further information, please call 1-800-793-9396.

Printed in United States by Versa Press

20 19 18 17 16 15 14 13 12 11 10 9 8

Library of Congress Cataloging-in-Publication Data

Neville, Kati.
 Fix, freeze, feast / Kati Neville and Lindsay Tkacsik.
  p. cm.
 Includes index.
 ISBN 978-1-58017-682-8 (hardcover : alk. paper)
 1. Ready meals. I. Tkacsik, Lindsay. II. Title.
TX833.5.N48 2007
641.5'55—dc22

2007033455

CONTENTS

WAREHOUSE SHOPPING, FAMILY COOKING

Even with all the recipe books, cooking classes, how-to manuals, and television programs devoted to the subject of meal preparation, many of us still find ourselves hungry and disorganized by the time the dinner hour rolls around. There is no end to the excellent resources available, but our busy lives get the better of us, and all our good intentions can come to naught. We want to feed our families healthful, economical meals that taste great and do not require hours of work. How can we accomplish this when time is short and the demands of work and family are ever increasing?

How are you coping? Is the local pizza delivery outfit on speed dial? Do you rely on drive-through fast food, expensive restaurant meals, packaged convenience foods, uninspired, boring food thrown together in a hurry? Maybe you're ready to try something new but don't know where to start.

This book will help you. Contained within these pages are dozens of fabulous recipes for dishes you can prepare in advance. Freeze them and pull one out at a moment's notice — you'll be rewarded with a delicious dinner you made from scratch without spending hours in the kitchen!

Warehouse clubs are everywhere, and they are among the best places to save money, day in and day out, on many products. True, if you are willing to chase down the bargains, they can be had in other places as well, but for many busy families, the warehouse is the place to go for major shopping trips.

The large size of the packages at the warehouse can be intimidating, though. Do you linger in the meat department, attracted by the competitive prices but wondering what you would ever do with so much meat? Maybe you've bought a large package of boneless chicken breasts, planning to split the contents into smaller portions to freeze for later.

We've heard from people who have bought a warehouse pack intending to defrost a few breasts at a time for family dinners. But, despite the good intentions, it usually goes something like this: After hours of running errands, your last stop is the warehouse store, where you notice the chicken is much cheaper than at the supermarket so you buy a package. You finally get home, the kids are getting off the bus, hungry and impatient. The baby's crying and has a soggy diaper, and you still have to unload the groceries and get dinner started. You throw the chicken into the fridge and notice it there a few days later. Worried there's no time to spare, you toss the whole big package into the freezer. Result: you're stuck with a six-pound solid sheet of chicken and don't know what to do with it!

If not that scenario exactly, you might regularly buy the warehouse packs of meat, knowing they're a great way to save money, and split them into single-meal sizes before freezing them. The only problem is, when dinnertime approaches, you have a frozen chunk of meat and no good ideas for what to do with it. There has to be a better way! If these experiences sound something like yours, you have the right resource in hand. Read on!

We have created our recipes based on the large packages of meat from warehouse clubs — the tray packs. We developed the Tray Pack Method to help people just like you! The Tray Pack Method allows you to fix several meals at one time. No doubt you're used to preparing a recipe from start to finish and then presenting a hot meal to your family. But our method is different: we scale the recipe to the warehouse tray pack of meat and then divide it into multiple meals. The meals are prepared right up to the final cooking stage. You then package and freeze them, and voilà — all you have to do is thaw one and cook it for dinner! It couldn't be easier, especially with these tasty recipes and our proven system to get you started.

Not only is our system straightforward, but it's also flexible. If you have only two hours every other week to prepare a few entrées, simply select two recipes that use the meat from two tray packs. Even this small step will yield several entrées. Devote a day and make six recipes that use six tray packs and yield many more entrées. By cooking the tray-pack way, you have the flexibility and control to prepare as many entrées as your time and energy allow.

Maybe you have already read articles or books on cooking ahead and filling your freezer. Admittedly, ours is not the first recipe book touting the benefits of using your freezer to keep ready-made food on hand. On our own bookshelves we have cookbooks featuring meals for the freezer that date back to the 1950s.

But what we offer here that's new and unique is a method that's updated to the modern warehouse shopping experience while preserving the proven benefits of storing main dish meals and other items in the freezer.

We know what it's like to balance children, jobs, activities, and a household. As owners of meal-preparation businesses, we bring you our best of the best in this book. Yes, these recipes are straight from our stash — tried, tested, and true. Our clients have made many of these recipes countless times and rave about the delicious results. We are passionate about what we do and uncompromising in our commitment to using fresh, from-scratch ingredients wherever possible. We give you only dishes that meet the same standard we use to feed our own families and those of our customers.

Whether you're a novice or an advanced cook, a bargain shopper or someone with money to spare, time-starved or a leisurely from-scratch cook, you'll find here recipes and tips that will help you create wonderful meals without a lot of work!

BECOMING A WAREHOUSE GOURMET

Begin by evaluating how busy you are and what your family currently likes to eat. Do you need an entrée every night of the week, or will you still cook from scratch some of the time? Are you preparing for company, expecting a baby, or anticipating an interruption in your routine?

If you're new to make ahead meals, we suggest you start with one or two recipes at first. Consider choosing a recipe for a simple marinade poured over meat — a quick and delicious way to acquaint yourself with our method. Tequila-Lime Chicken, Honey-Glazed Chicken Thighs, An's Pork Chops, and Basil-Balsamic Chops, are simple meals for beginners. Or you may want to look for recipes that are similar to dinner dishes you currently prepare. It never hurts to go with the tried-and-true.

If you already "batch-cook," belong to a dinner co-op, or practice other forms of advance meal preparation, these recipes will work nicely with your current practices. Even if you have experience, we still recommend you start off with a few different recipes and gradually increase the number you do in a session to meet your needs — although we recommend doing no more than six at a time. The purpose of this book is to make feeding your family easier. No need for crazy marathon cooking sessions that leave you wondering what on earth you were thinking!

Following are just a few of the benefits you will enjoy when you fix, freeze, and feast.

ECONOMY: Every time you eat from your freezer you save money, especially if it takes the place of frequently eating out.

TIME MANAGEMENT: If you normally shop daily and cook one meal at a time, we estimate our method will save you an hour or more every day.

CONVENIENCE: Things come up: There are evenings when everyone in the family is busy; late or unplanned meetings cut into cooking time; children's school friends or other unexpected company stop by; a friend is in need. It is wonderful to have a few meals on hand, for every day or just in case.

ADAPTABILITY: If you watch what you eat — for whatever reason — pre-prepared meals will help you stay on track.

VARIETY: An interesting selection of freezer meals integrated with fresh meals and the occasional restaurant treat will prevent food boredom.

FUN: Work through your recipes with a friend or two. Sharing stories and laughter makes the time seem less like work and more like play.

ACCOMPLISHMENT: It's a wonderful feeling to have nourishing food in the freezer and an organized and efficient approach to daily dinners.

Most of the recipes in this book are for entrées, but don't miss the other gems! We have included an assortment of brunch items, side dishes, snacks, sweets, and sauces. We offer a selection of meatless recipes and even some handmade spice mixes sprinkled throughout the chapters. Fill your freezer with main dishes or the extras — either way, you'll enjoy all the benefits of make-ahead meals.

Let's get started!

PLANNING FOR SUCCESS

To be successful, start with a plan. Even if it's just a mental list of steps you'll take, thinking through what you want to accomplish will keep you organized and efficient. We have broken our Tray Pack Method into a few simple steps.

THE BASICS OF MAKE-AHEAD MEALS

1. Get Organized! Every session begins with a plan, which includes a shopping list and a prep list. Divide yours between warehouse and grocery store items for easy reference.

2. Consolidate ingredients common to several recipes. Be sure you know exactly what you need and where to find everything before you go shopping.

3. Go Shopping! Take your list and buy your groceries. Don't forget your membership cards.

4. Follow your prep list to chop, dice, and otherwise organize your ingredients. When all your items are ready to go, you can begin the recipes.

5. Label bags, assemble recipes, and freeze.

6. Heat & Eat! Thaw entrées as you need weeknight meals. Once defrosted, you can quickly prepare home-cooked meals for your family – even on the busiest nights!

1. GET ORGANIZED! MAKING YOUR SHOPPING LIST

Make a shopping list of the ingredients used in each recipe you intend to prepare. We suggest writing every ingredient down, even if you know you have it on hand. Once your list is complete, go through the kitchen and mark off the items you already have. Now you know exactly what to buy at the store, and you also have a complete list from which to work when you begin your session. We buy almost all our ingredients from warehouse clubs and local grocery stores. Different shopping destinations require separate lists: Put the items you will get at the warehouse club in one column; put those you'll pick up at the supermarket in another.

We find it helpful to divide shopping lists further according to food type: meat, dairy, vegetables, seasonings, dry goods, canned goods, and so on. Keep in mind that some warehouse stores get thousands of shoppers on a weekend day. If this is the only time you can shop at the warehouse, we recommend that you divide your list according to food type so that you can move more efficiently through the crowded aisles.

Don't forget to keep those shopping lists even after you've finished all your shopping. They will be useful as you gather everything for your cooking session.

2. SELECTING INGREDIENTS

Our recipe ingredients usually begin with the tray pack meat or other warehouse product. We have found that the various warehouse clubs across the country sell their meat in similar size packages. In our recipes we give a weight approximation in case package sizes vary or you decide to buy your meat elsewhere. Try to begin with total weights close to the amount called for in the recipe, but don't worry if you're bit over or under. The recipes are flexible enough to accommodate small differences.

All other ingredients can be found at the warehouse or the supermarket. Buy ingredients at the warehouse only if you can use the entire amount before the expiration date; otherwise, buy smaller packages at the grocery store. There is no sense in buying more of an ingredient than you will use. It isn't a bargain if it's wasted!

Both warehouse clubs and grocery stores offer ingredients in various states of preparation to make things easier on the cook. You can buy shredded cheese instead of bricks of cheese, peeled garlic cloves instead of whole heads of garlic, and chopped onion instead of whole onions. Before you choose an item, you'll want to consider the quantity you need, the preparation time you'll save, and how much more you'll pay for the convenience. Choose what will work best for you and your budget without compromising quality.

If an ingredient sounds unfamiliar and you are unsure if your local grocer carries it, call ahead and save yourself the trouble of running from store to store. Ask a service clerk to help you locate an item; it may be in an unexpected area. Occasionally one of our recipes calls for a specialty ingredient. When that is the case, we will let you know in the recipe directions how you can obtain it or what you can substitute.

Some common ingredients are available in several forms. We have chosen to list them one way throughout the book. Following is a list of common items with our preferred form and possible substitutions.

CHICKEN OR BEEF BOUILLON GRANULES: There are several ways to buy bouillon; we prefer bouillon without monosodium glutamate (MSG). Our recipes call for 1 teaspoon of bouillon granules to equal 1 cup of reconstituted broth. Some bouillon cubes and base are more or less concentrated, so read labels carefully to determine the correct amount to use depending on the form you've selected.

GARLIC: We prefer the freshness and flavor of mincing fresh garlic cloves. Use a chopper, food processor, knife, or garlic press. Bottled minced garlic is an acceptable substitute and is easy to measure out in large quantities.

GINGER: Peel and chop fresh gingerroot before mincing it in a food processor or mini chopper. It's well worth the effort of using fresh ginger for the superior flavor it imparts to the recipes.

ONION: In our recipes, "onion" refers to fresh onion, peeled and chopped, or minced in a food processor or mini chopper. If the recipe requires any other form — dried onion flakes, for example — the recipe will so indicate. Our recipes call for fresh onion to be chopped, diced, or minced. Chop and dice onion with a knife or food processor. Chopped pieces are roughly double the size of diced. Mincing is best done in a food processor, as it cuts the onion very fine, just short of a purée.

BREADCRUMBS: Our recipes using breadcrumbs all call for dry bread crumbs. If not otherwise specified, choose either seasoned or plain.

BLACK PEPPER: Unless otherwise indicated, use any form you like — cracked, crushed, or ground.

CRUSHED RED PEPPER: In some stores, the container may say "red pepper flakes."

SCALLIONS: In some stores, scallions are called green onions.

VEGETABLE COOKING SPRAY: The cooking directions in each relevant recipe indicate whether a baking dish is greased or ungreased. Please note that "greased" does not necessarily refer to the use of butter or oil but can also mean using a vegetable cooking spray.

We have included an example of what a completed shopping list and prep list for several recipes might look like in the appendix on pages 218 and 219.

3. GO SHOPPING!

 You've made a detailed shopping list and it's time to get out there and purchase your supplies. But before you go, clear ample space in your refrigerator for the perishable groceries you'll be bringing home. Whether you find shopping a necessary evil or something to enjoy, there are several things you should take along, as listed below.

A COOLER FILLED WITH ICE IF THE WEATHER IS HOT: You don't want to buy 20 pounds of meat only to have it spoil in the car because your errands took longer than expected or you got caught in traffic.

YOUR SHOPPING AND PREP LISTS: Double-check that you have your lists before you leave the house. You may want to secure them to a small clipboard for easy reference and to write on as you shop.

CLUB CARDS: Remember to take your warehouse membership card and your supermarket club cards, too. You're not shopping for supermarket bargains now, but in the event that you encounter a sale, you'll be glad you're prepared so you can take advantage of the savings.

THIS BOOK! If a question arises or a last-minute decision needs to be made, you can refer to our instructions while shopping.

Food Safety: Take care that your packages of raw meat do not accidentally contaminate your other groceries. Most warehouse clubs and grocery stores make plastic bags available to pack your meat separately from the rest of your groceries. We recommend you use these bags. When stacking your purchases in the grocery cart, cooler, or refrigerator, place meat on the bottom so that if a leak occurs, the juice will not drip on other foods.

4. FIX AND FREEZE! SETTING UP YOUR KITCHEN

A clean and tidy kitchen is important for an organized and successful cooking session. Before you begin, empty the sink and dishwasher, clear the counter-tops, and have a large, empty trash can handy. If you're planning to prepare several recipes at once, try to have some space cleared in your freezer so you don't have to stop and shuffle things around to make room for your packages.

The shopping lists you made are a complete list of ingredients for the session. Set the nonperishables on the counter. It's more efficient to do this ahead rather than locating one thing at a time during the session.

Have all your equipment handy. Keep in mind that when cooking recipes with large yields, the bowls, skillets, and pots need to be large enough to accommodate the ingredients. Get out the big stuff!

It's not necessary to own every fancy, expensive gadget. If you don't have everything you need in your own kitchen, ask a friend or family member to lend you equipment. As far as material goes, we prefer stainless steel to glass or plastic. Glass is heavy and breakable and plastic can be difficult to clean. The following is a list of items we suggest you have on hand:

- Extra measuring cups and spoons
- Large liquid measuring cup with a spout
- Large stainless steel bowls
- Very large stockpot (8-quart capacity or larger)
- Various sizes of sauté pans and saucepans
- Whisks, wooden mixing spoons, and nonstick spatulas
- Good-quality sharp knives, at least one per cook
- Basic first aid kit (Even the best cooks get an occasional burn or nick!)
- A variety of dishwasher-safe cutting boards to keep meat and produce separate

- Rimmed baking sheets
- Boxes, containers, or cans for holding your bags open and steady for easy filling (Refer to the packaging and freezing tips on page 15.)
- Splatter screen
- Small food chopper or a food processor (Mini food choppers can be found at a reasonable price and are sufficient for mincing garlic, onions, and ginger, and for chopping nuts.)
- Lemon zester (This tool is helpful for removing the colored part of citrus rind from the fruit without getting any of the white pith underneath. There are many versions of this tool that work well. The very small holes on a box grater will do in a pinch.)
- Cookie scoop (Use for both cookies and meatballs.)
- Pot holders, hot pads, and/or trivets
- Extra dish towels
- Countertop disinfectant
- Tape and permanent fine markers

PREP YOUR INGREDIENTS

Our recipes call for ingredients in a "ready-to-go" state. This means the ingredient list includes brief instructions for readying the items to be added to the dish. In the Teriyaki Chicken recipe, for example, the phrase "skin removed" is in the ingredient list, directly after the chicken thigh listing. Further down, the recipe calls for minced garlic and minced ginger. These recipe ready cues indicate that you should remove the skin and mince both the garlic and ginger before you begin making the recipe.

It can be helpful to make a list of preparation steps for each recipe on the back of the shopping list. One consolidated list helps to readily identify opportunities to combine tasks wherever possible. For instance, if two recipes call for chopped onion, combine the quantities and chop enough onion for both recipes at once. Having one sheet of paper with both shopping and prep lists is also convenient. It's available for quick reference out at the store and then again back in the kitchen.

5. PUTTING IT ALL TOGETHER

 You've made it! You've planned, shopped, and chopped. You're almost ready to begin with the first recipe you selected. Now is also the time to create labels for the food you will be preparing. After completing your preparation tasks, get out the number of freezer bags you'll need and label them all before moving through each recipe. It's much easier to label flat bags than filled ones. Labels for baking dishes can be affixed to or written directly on the wrap. Labeling your entrées is the only way to avoid "freezer surprise" — that dreaded freezer meal without a name or date to indicate how long it has been in there. There are different labeling options available to you; some are listed below.

- The appendix contains sample labels for your convenience. You can photocopy the labels you need and tape them to your freezer containers. Our labels are printed with baking instructions, times, and temperatures. For easy reference, we have also noted any additional ingredients that you'll need to have on hand. Use permanent markers to write the date on the label or directly on the freezer bag.
- If you know you'll be keeping all the meals for yourself, use a permanent marker to write the date, recipe name, and page number on the bag. This allows you to refer to the book for the cooking instructions.
- You can also go to the *Fix, Freeze, Feast* page at www.storey.com and print PDFs of the labels on Avery stickers. The online templates work with Avery labels

(types 5265, 5165, 8165, 8665, 8465, 8255), available wherever office supplies are sold.

With all your freezer bags labeled and your ingredients prepped and ready in the kitchen, you can put it all together. In preparing our recipes, we encourage you to experiment. If you want to use less liquor than what's called for, do so. Add more garlic. Use more vegetables. Try to incorporate some of your family's preferences into your preparation. While you do so, make notes so you can remember what you did in order to duplicate your successes.

Second Generation Recipes: You will notice that several recipes in this book are grouped together and marked with our Second Generation recipe stamp. These meals are intended to be eaten without being frozen first and are the offspring of a few of our favorite recipes.

For example, Dave's Swamp Blues Barbeque Chicken is a typical tray pack recipe that yields three entrées. The "Second Generation" recipes that follow it show you how to take one of those entrées and prepare it for use in either of these two fresh recipes: Dave's Skillet Hash or Dave's Barbecued Chicken Pizza. Second Generation recipes are a great way to add more mealtime variety while extending the economy and convenience of our make-ahead meals.

One of the most important things to remember as you prepare our recipes is that you must never pour a hot sauce over raw meat. To avoid food-borne illness, hot food should be kept above 140°F and cold food should be kept below 40°F. Anywhere in between is considered a danger zone, conducive to bacterial growth. You will need to cool all hot sauces before they can be added to raw meats. To be safe, do this as quickly as possible. When a recipe indicates you should cool a sauce, this is the proper way to do it: Pour the hot sauce into a large shallow pan. Use more than one pan if necessary, as the sauce should not be more than 4 inches deep. Leave the pan uncovered. Place the pan in the sink and carefully add cold water and ice around the pan until the water reaches the outside rim. Stir the sauce in the pan frequently. When the sauce reaches 70°F, you can transfer it to the refrigerator to keep it cool until it's used in the recipe. **Never pour a hot sauce over raw meat.**

Food Safety: You may rarely think about food-borne illness in your day to day cooking. In all likelihood you are already practicing good food safety – washing your hands frequently, keeping raw meat separate from vegetables and condiments, and cleaning up spills promptly. When working with large volumes of food, be even more scrupulous. Use hot, soapy water to clean equipment and cooking surfaces. Keep cold foods in the refrigerator or a cooler with ice until you're ready to use them in the recipe. Cool hot sauces according to our directions, and cook your foods to the appropriate temperatures.

CORRECTING MISTAKES

Every once in a while you'll discover you've made a mistake while preparing a recipe. Don't panic! In all our years of cooking for our families and with groups in our businesses, we've encountered only a few mistakes that couldn't be fixed. The rest we were able to repair and, in some cases, preferred the "wrong" version!

We've designed our method to help you avoid mistakes in the first place. We've tested for the intensity of seasonings, how reliably an entrée comes together in your kitchen, and how well it retains its quality in the freezer. Nevertheless, mistakes still happen, and in order to avoid having to throw away food, here are some suggestions in case you face a kitchen quandary.

HOW CAN I FIX MY RECIPE IF I . . .

MEASURE AN INGREDIENT INCORRECTLY? If you add too much of one ingredient, often you can simply increase the whole recipe proportionately. See our tips on adapting recipes (page 212) for some rules of thumb.

If you put too much of a dry ingredient into a mix and it's sitting on top of other ingredients or floating on top of a marinade, try to scoop off the excess. Chances are, you'll be able to approximate the original amount.

FORGET TO USE AN INGREDIENT? If you're all finished and find an unused ingredient on the counter, determine where you made the error and whether or not it will be easy to add. In a marinade, for example, you can simply add the correct amount to each bag before freezing. Alternatively, you can add it to the entrée when it comes out of the freezer, but remember to make a note of it on the label.

BUY THE WRONG MEAT? Sometimes you'll find you end up with a cut of meat you didn't mean to buy. The package may have been placed in the wrong section of the cooler and picked up inadvertently. One of our customers accidentally bought pork instead of beef for the Beef Barley Soup. She ended up making Pork Barley Soup and it was great. If the recipe can be adapted for the cut of meat, go ahead and use it anyway; otherwise, just pick another recipe to use with the meat that you took home.

FIND SOMETHING TOO SALTY? Salt is an ingredient that intensifies in strength in the freezer. We write our recipes to account for this, but different brands of bouillon and other seasonings can vary in saltiness. Individual tastes differ, too.

If a sauce or marinade tastes too salty to you before it goes into the freezer, you can make the sauce again, this time omitting all salt or bouillon that the recipe calls for. Mix the two sauces together. You can use the same method for a marinade, or you can add plain chicken broth or apple juice a teaspoonful at a time until the saltiness has been diluted. *Please don't taste sauces or marinades that contain raw meat!*

FIND THERE'S TOO MUCH FLAVOR? Like salt, vinegar and alcohol can impart a strong, pronounced flavor. If you decide there's too strong a vinegar or alcohol flavor for your taste, adding plain chicken broth, apple juice, or water will help balance the dish.

FIND THERE'S NOT ENOUGH FLAVOR? If you taste something before it goes into the freezer and think its flavor should be stronger, resist the temptation to doctor the seasonings. Many flavors intensify in the freezer. If you need to, you can adjust the seasoning when you cook the entrée.

BREAK OR TEAR A FREEZER BAG? Breakage is rare, and there are simple ways to keep your freezer bags intact. Hot sauces can weaken a freezer bag; that's another reason we advise you always to cool food before placing it in a bag. Bags full of sauce or soup tend to freeze into very hard packages, so it's best to move them very little once they're frozen.

If you damage a bag before an entrée has been frozen, carefully transfer the contents to a new freezer bag. If you discover a tear in a bag after the food has been frozen, put the whole entrée, broken bag and all, into a new freezer bag.

FORGET TO PUT FOOD INTO THE REFRIGERATOR/FREEZER? This one can be a heartbreaker. We've heard a few stories from cooks who inadvertently left an entrée on the counter too long. Perishable food must be stored at a temperature below 40°F, or it is considered unsafe to consume. Please do not risk your health; throw away any food that has not been held at a safe temperature.

SOMETIMES A MISTAKE LEADS TO A NEW FAVORITE: Sometimes you don't realize your error until it's too late. While testing recipes, both of us made mistakes measuring ingredients. We had to laugh at our rookie errors, but we were pleased to find that some new versions turned out better than the originals.

HELPFUL TIPS FOR PACKAGING AND FREEZING

Carefully packaging and freezing your entrées will ensure the best quality when it comes to dinner time. Here are some tips.

WHAT IS THE BEST WAY TO . . .

POUR SAUCE INTO FREEZER BAGS? This can be a messy procedure. Here's what we've found works best: Save cracker boxes, large plastic sour cream or cottage cheese tubs, or the enormous #10 cans (such as those used in the Basic Red Sauce recipe), being careful to leave a smooth edge when removing the lid. Put the freezer bag inside one of these containers and fold the top of the bag over the rim of the container. This will hold your bag open and prevent spills while you measure or pour in ingredients.

MIX MARINADES? Many of the marinades can be made in a large, clear liquid measuring cup instead of a bowl. This will help take the guesswork out when dividing the sauce among the bags.

STORE THE FINISHED ENTRÉES? We recommend always using heavy-duty freezer bags. Don't use regular storage bags. Our recipes most often call for 1-quart and 1-gallon freezer bags, which are available in bulk at the warehouse store. Two-gallon and 1-pint freezer bags are called for occasionally and can be found at the grocery store.

PREVENT ICE CRYSTALS? Remove as much air as possible from each bag before sealing and placing it in the freezer. This will increase the freezer life of the food and keep ice crystals from forming.

AVOID LEAKS? If you're packaging meat with bones, such as pork chops or ribs, double-bag the entrée to help avoid leaks. Simply fill the first freezer bag and seal it. Then place the sealed bag inside a second bag. Label the outer bag.

PACKAGE MEALS TO GIVE AWAY? If the recipe calls for a baking dish, you can use your own glass or metal pans. But if you decide to give a meal away, it can be a bother for both you and the recipient to worry about the container's return. In that case, you may wish to use a disposable foil pan. Think carefully about the intended use of the meals you choose and plan to package them accordingly.

FREEZE THE CORRECT PORTIONS? Package your items according to the recipes, or, alternatively, to suit the size of your family. If you have a small family, you may want to divide entrées into smaller portions before freezing. Or you might want to divide the portions as we suggest and plan to have leftovers.

KEEP TRACK OF WHAT'S IN THE FREEZER? Keep a freezer inventory. Maintain it so you know at a glance what you have in the freezer. See the appendix for a form you can use to keep track of the contents of your freezer.

A QUESTION YOU MIGHT ASK: I have limited space in my freezer — can I still use this method? Don't worry, this method will work even for cooks with limited freezer space. You may be surprised at how much food can fit in a standard freezer. Following are some tips for conserving freezer space.

- Choose recipes for dishes that will be stored in plastic freezer bags rather than in baking dishes. Freeze these entrées flat; once frozen, line them up vertically (as you would books on a shelf).

- Make only one or two recipes at a time.

- Pick recipes with lower yields. Stick to those recipes that make two or three entrées each rather than those that yield larger numbers.

- Consider trading entrées with a friend to maximize variety while conserving freezer space (see our community cooking suggestions, page 214).

Freezer Burn: The result of moisture loss from poorly packaged food, freezer burn creates a fuzzy and grayish-white surface on the frozen item. It's not harmful, but it can result in an undesirable flavor and texture. Prevent freezer burn by following our freezing tips. Ice crystals are different from freezer burn. Their appearance has to do with how quickly the food has frozen. A cold freezer will create small ice crystals, and the smaller the crystals, the less they will diminish food quality. The ideal freezer temperature is between -5 and 0°F.

6. HEAT AND EAT! THAWING AND COOKING

We specify in every recipe that you should completely thaw your frozen items in the refrigerator — not on the counter and never in a hot-water bath. Always thaw your food in the refrigerator. Correctly thawing meat and cooking it to appropriate temperatures are the best way to avoid food-borne illness. Skip thawing in the refrigerator only when a recipe indicates that the item can go directly from the freezer to the oven.

Cook all meat to the temperature indicated in the directions. Some meats' temperatures will continue to rise after you remove it from the oven or grill, so you may remove the meat from the heat source when it is a few degrees below the indicated temperature as long as you are sure it will reach the required temperature before it is eaten.

Once an entrée has been thawed, you must cook it. Never thaw raw meat and then refreeze it. As the saying goes: When in doubt, throw it out!

As for the cooking methods, we have listed what we find works best for each recipe. It's up to you if you want to alter the method. You may choose to bake a dish for which the recipe calls for grilling, or use the slow cooker instead of the oven. In many cases, an alternative cooking method will work well, but if you want to be sure of success, use the cooking method specified in the recipe.

CHAPTER ONE

CHICKEN MAIN DISHES

This chicken is excellent chopped over salad with red grapes, blue cheese, and sunflower seeds. Consider dressing the salad with our Raspberry Vinaigrette (page 186). Fresh or frozen sweet cherries in place of the raspberries bring out the cherry flavor of the chicken. —KN

CHERRY SKILLET CHICKEN

MAKES 3 ENTRÉES, 4 SERVINGS EACH

1 TRAY (ABOUT 6 POUNDS) BONELESS, SKINLESS CHICKEN HALF-BREASTS

1½ cups (9 ounces) chopped dried sweet cherries

1 cup hot water

1½ cups chicken broth

6 tablespoons white balsamic vinegar or white wine vinegar

3 teaspoons sugar

¾ teaspoon sea salt

Wax paper

3 one-gallon freezer bags, labeled

ON HAND FOR COOKING EACH ENTRÉE

2 teaspoons vegetable oil

1. Rinse and trim chicken as desired.

2. Lay each piece of chicken, smooth side down, between two sheets of wax paper. Using a rolling pin or a meat tenderizer, pound each chicken piece to 1 inch thick. Divide chicken evenly among the three freezer bags.

3. Put cherries in a small bowl and cover with hot water. Let stand for 5 minutes.

4. Measure ½ cup chicken broth, 2 tablespoons vinegar, 1 teaspoon sugar, and ¼ teaspoon salt into each freezer bag with chicken.

5. Drain cherries. Divide cherries equally into the freezer bags with the chicken. Seal and gently shake bag to distribute cherries.

6. Freeze.

TO COOK ONE ENTRÉE

1. Completely thaw one entrée in the refrigerator.

2. Heat oil in a large skillet over medium heat. Add the chicken and cook until it begins to brown, about 3 minutes on each side.

3. Reduce heat to medium-low and pour cherries and juice over chicken. Cover and simmer 12 to 15 minutes, or until an instant-read thermometer inserted into the thickest part of the chicken reads 170°F.

SWEET CHERRIES

According to the Cherry Marketing Institute, there are over a thousand sweet cherry varieties. Notable national varieties such as Bing, Rainier, Chelan, or Black Tartarian are among the easiest to find locally.

This is based on a casserole I used to make with cream of chicken soup. My condensed soup days are over, but we still like this dish. In fact, it has become a family favorite, perfect for nights when we're on the run. Serve over brown basmati rice for extra nutrition. —LT

CHICKEN-BROCCOLI BAKE

MAKES 3 ENTRÉES, 4–6 SERVINGS EACH

1 TRAY (ABOUT 6 POUNDS) BONELESS, SKINLESS CHICKEN HALF-BREASTS

½ cup (1 stick) butter

1 pound fresh white mushrooms, cleaned and sliced

¾ cup all-purpose flour

1 tablespoon chicken bouillon granules

1 tablespoon curry powder

¾ teaspoon black pepper

2 cups water

4 cups milk

2 tablespoons lemon juice

6 cups broccoli pieces (about 1¼ pounds), washed

6 cups shredded Cheddar cheese (about 1½ pounds)

1½ cups dry bread crumbs

6 one-gallon freezer bags, label 3

3 one-quart freezer bags

1. Rinse and trim chicken as desired. Cut chicken into bite-size pieces and cook in a large skillet over medium heat until no longer pink, about 30 minutes. Remove from heat and cool. Divide cooled chicken evenly among the three unlabeled 1-gallon freezer bags.

2. While chicken cools, melt butter in a separate large saucepan over medium heat. Add mushrooms and sauté until softened, about 5 minutes. Add flour and stir. Mixture will be lumpy. Cook, stirring, for 2 minutes. Add bouillon, curry powder, and pepper; stir. Gradually add water and milk; cook, stirring constantly, until sauce thickens, about 10 minutes. Whisk to make a smooth sauce. Add lemon juice only after sauce has thickened. Cool sauce.

3. Divide cooled sauce evenly over the chicken. Measure 2 cups of broccoli pieces into each bag of chicken and sauce. Seal bags.

4. Measure 2 cups cheese and ½ cup breadcrumbs into each of the three 1-quart freezer bags. Seal bags.

5. Place one bag of chicken/broccoli and one bag of cheese/breadcrumb mixture into each labeled 1-gallon bag.

6. Seal and freeze.

TO COOK ONE ENTRÉE

1. Completely thaw one entrée in the refrigerator.

2. Preheat the oven to 350°F.

3. Place chicken and broccoli mixture in an ungreased baking dish and sprinkle with cheese and breadcrumbs. Bake, uncovered, for 35 to 40 minutes, or until the sauce is bubbling and the cheese is melted.

BE PREPARED

Notice something different? When you read these recipes, you'll notice they are presented differently from those in a typical cookbook. Because these entrées go straight to the freezer, all the components of the meal are packaged together to eliminate last-minute dinner hassles.

Chicken, ham, and cheese — what's not to like? When my children were very young, they would split one of these three ways: Ellen ate the chicken, Laura ate the ham, and Natalie ate the cheese! —LT

CHICKEN CORDON BLEU

MAKES 12 ROLLS

1 TRAY (ABOUT 6 POUNDS) BONELESS, SKINLESS CHICKEN HALF-BREASTS

1 cup all-purpose flour

4 eggs, lightly beaten

2 cups dry bread crumbs

12 slices Swiss cheese

12 slices deli ham

Wax paper

Plastic wrap

3 one-gallon freezer bags, labeled

ON HAND FOR COOKING EACH ENTRÉE

2 teaspoons melted butter per chicken roll

1. Rinse and trim chicken as desired.

2. Lay out three shallow dishes. Measure the flour into one, eggs into another, and breadcrumbs into the third.

3. Lay each piece of chicken, smooth side down, between two sheets of wax paper. Using a rolling pin or a meat tenderizer, pound each chicken piece to ½ inch thick. Take one piece of chicken, coat with flour, dip in egg, and then coat with breadcrumbs. Set aside. Repeat with remaining chicken pieces. Discard remaining flour, egg, and breadcrumbs.

4. Fold one piece of cheese into a small bundle and place in the middle of one slice of ham. Fold the sides of the ham in, enveloping the cheese. Place a ham/cheese bundle on the narrow end of a breaded chicken piece, roll chicken into a packet, and secure tightly by wrapping with plastic wrap. Repeat with remaining cheese, ham, and chicken. Divide chicken rolls evenly among the freezer bags.

5. Seal and freeze.

TO COOK ONE ENTRÉE

1. Remove desired number of chicken rolls from freezer. Discard plastic wrap while chicken is still frozen and place rolls in a greased baking dish. Place in the refrigerator to thaw completely.

2. Preheat the oven to 350°F.

3. Brush each chicken roll with 2 teaspoons melted butter and bake for 45 minutes, or until an instant read thermometer inserted into the thickest part of the chicken reads 170°F.

TOOTHPICKS?

Some rolled chicken breast recipes call for toothpicks to secure the bundles. I don't recommend that method for this recipe because toothpicks don't do a very good job of sealing these up tightly enough to prevent the cheese from leaking out. If you wrap each serving securely with plastic wrap, taking care to pull in the ends to create a snug bundle, it should stay together on its own when it comes out of the freezer.

This mild and creamy curry is a hit with everyone. If you're not sure whether your family will eat curry, I suggest you start here. —LT

CHICKEN CURRY

MAKES 3 ENTRÉES, 4–6 SERVINGS EACH

1 TRAY (ABOUT 6 POUNDS) BONELESS, SKINLESS CHICKEN HALF-BREASTS

1 cup (2 sticks) butter

2 cups chopped onion (about 2 medium)

¼ cup curry powder

2 tablespoons minced ginger

2 tablespoons minced garlic (about 18 cloves)

2 tablespoons sugar

2 tablespoons chicken bouillon granules

2 teaspoons salt

1 cup all-purpose flour

4 cups water

4 cups milk

2 tablespoons lemon juice

3 one-gallon freezer bags, labeled

1. Rinse and trim chicken as desired. Cut chicken into bite-size pieces and cook in a large skillet over medium heat until no longer pink, about 30 minutes. Remove from heat and cool. Divide cooled chicken evenly among freezer bags.

2. While chicken cools, melt butter in a separate large saucepan over medium heat. Add onions and cook, stirring, until soft, about 5 minutes. Add curry powder, ginger, garlic, sugar, bouillon, and salt; cook, stirring, for 2 minutes. Add flour and cook, stirring, 2 minutes longer. Mixture will be like a paste. Gradually add the water and milk; cook, stirring constantly, until the sauce has thickened. Whisk to make a smooth sauce. Add lemon juice only after sauce has thickened. Cool sauce.

3. Divide cooled sauce evenly over the chicken.

4. Seal and freeze.

TO COOK ONE ENTRÉE

1. Completely thaw one entrée in the refrigerator.

2. In a large skillet over medium heat, bring the chicken and curry sauce to a simmer and cook until heated through. Do not boil.

3. Serve curry over your favorite rice.

ACCOMPANIMENTS FOR CURRY

Arrange a platter of toppings so your guests can select their favorite flavors to sprinkle over dinner. The platter could include: toasted coconut, toasted almonds, fresh apple pieces, pineapple tidbits, raisins, dried cranberries, chopped scallions, mango chutney, hot chili paste, and/or sweet chili sauce.

Many recipes for this dish call for frying the chicken. I find that messy and time-consuming, so I developed this baked version. This entrée pairs nicely with your favorite pasta and a little extra red sauce. —LT

CHICKEN PARMIGIANA

MAKES 3 ENTRÉES, 4 SERVINGS EACH

1 TRAY (ABOUT 6 POUNDS) BONELESS, SKINLESS CHICKEN HALF-BREASTS

1 cup all-purpose flour

4 eggs, lightly beaten

2 cups dry bread crumbs

12 slices mozzarella cheese

6 cups Basic Red Sauce (page 178)

Plastic wrap

3 one-gallon freezer bags, labeled

3 one-quart freezer bags

1. Rinse and trim chicken as desired. Lay out three shallow dishes. Measure the flour into one, eggs into another, and breadcrumbs into the third.

2. Slightly flatten the chicken by laying each piece, smooth side down, on your cutting board, and using the palm of your hand to press down on the thickest part of the chicken. Take one piece of chicken, coat with flour, dip in egg, and then coat with breadcrumbs. Repeat with remaining chicken pieces. Place coated chicken in one layer on a rimmed baking sheet.

3. When all chicken is coated, place in the freezer for 1 hour. Discard remaining flour, egg, and breadcrumbs.

4. Into each 1-quart freezer bag, measure 2 cups red sauce. Seal.

5. Divide cheese into three portions of 4 slices each; wrap in plastic wrap. Divide frozen chicken evenly among the 1-gallon freezer bags. Place one bag sauce and one packet of cheese into each bag of chicken.

6. Seal and freeze.

TO COOK ONE ENTRÉE

1. Completely thaw one entrée in the refrigerator.

2. Preheat the oven to 375°F.

3. Place chicken in a greased baking dish. Bake, uncovered, for 20 minutes. Pour red sauce evenly over each piece of chicken and continue baking for 10 minutes longer, or until an instant-read thermometer inserted into the thickest part of the chicken reads170°F. Place a slice of cheese on top of each piece of chicken and bake until melted.

I was working on a new barbecue sauce in the kitchen one Sunday afternoon when the radio program *This American Life* was playing swamp blues. The kitchen felt like the back porch instead of the back end of a greasy spoon for a change. I happened upon the right mix of ingredients to create a tangy new sauce. It was just the right thing for just the right lazy summer day. Following this recipe are two more that use this barbecued chicken as the main ingredient. —KN

DAVE'S SWAMP BLUES
BARBECUED CHICKEN

MAKES 3 ENTRÉES, 4 SERVINGS EACH

1 TRAY (ABOUT 6 POUNDS) BONELESS, SKINLESS CHICKEN HALF-BREASTS

2 teaspoons vegetable oil

1 cup chopped onion (about 1 medium)

2¼ cups ketchup

½ cup water

¼ cup bourbon

2 tablespoons lime juice

1 tablespoon smoked paprika

1 tablespoon brown sugar

4 teaspoons jerk seasoning (such as Penzeys, or try our handmade version on the following page)

3 one-gallon freezer bags, labeled

1. Heat oil in a large saucepan over medium heat. Add onion; cook, stirring, until soft, 2 to 3 minutes. Add ketchup, water, bourbon, lime juice, paprika, brown sugar, and jerk seasoning. Reduce heat; simmer 30 minutes, stirring frequently. Cool sauce.

2. While sauce is cooling, rinse and trim chicken as desired. Divide chicken evenly among the three freezer bags. Divide cooled sauce evenly over the chicken.

3. Seal and freeze.

TO COOK ONE ENTRÉE

1. Completely thaw one entrée in the refrigerator.

2. Prepare a medium-low fire in a gas or charcoal grill.

3. Grill chicken, turning every 5 minutes and basting frequently with the marinade, over medium-low heat for 30 minutes, or until an instant-read thermometer inserted into the thickest part of the chicken reads 170°F. Do not baste chicken during last 5 minutes of grilling.

HANDMADE JERK SEASONING

Making your own jerk seasoning is as easy as mixing together the following spices:

1 teaspoon cayenne pepper, 1 teaspoon ground allspice, ½ teaspoon black pepper, ½ teaspoon ground cinnamon, ½ teaspoon dried thyme, ½ teaspoon ground nutmeg

FAMILY MATTERS

My uncle Dave passed away in early 2005. I learned of his passing minutes before we met to work on this book. He loved to cook, too. I managed to rescue his Penzeys spice collection from the trash. Uncle Dave is the person who introduced me to their spices. The jerk seasoning I used in this recipe went straight from his cupboard to mine as my "inheritance." And so I dedicate this recipe to my uncle Dave, who called me "sparrow legs," tricked me into eating squirrel and rabbit, loved Elvis, cooked well, endured so much, and was loved by many. Including me.

I tried this recipe out on my dad several times before getting it right. My grandma used to make hash for him and his three brothers when he was a boy. Grandma's cooking was legendary in the family as well as in her township, where she and Grandpa Bill ran a tavern and eatery. I'm sure this hash isn't as good as hers — it's hard to compete with a son's memory of his mother's fine cooking, after all. Yet, Dave's Skillet Hash has managed to win his approval. —KN

DAVE'S SKILLET HASH

MAKES 6–8 SERVINGS

2 DAVE'S SWAMP BLUES BARBECUED CHICKEN HALF-BREASTS, GRILLED AND CHOPPED (PAGE 30)

1 tablespoon grapeseed oil

3½ cups (uncooked) cubed potatoes (about 1¼ pounds)

1 cup chopped onion (about 1 medium)

½ cup chopped green bell pepper

½ cup chopped red bell pepper

¾ cup chicken broth

1 teaspoon black pepper

½ teaspoon salt

½ teaspoon smoked paprika

¼ teaspoon crushed red pepper flakes

¾ cup shredded Cheddar cheese (about 3 ounces)

1. Heat oil in a deep skillet or Dutch oven over medium heat. Add potatoes and cook, stirring frequently, for 10 minutes. Add onion and green and red bell peppers; cook, stirring, 5 minutes longer. Pour in chicken broth. Sprinkle in black pepper, salt, paprika, and crushed red pepper and stir to combine.

2. Reduce heat, cover, and cook, stirring frequently, 10 to 15 minutes, or until the potatoes are soft. Add chicken, re-cover pan, and cook 5 minutes longer. Top with cheese and return pan to the oven. Serve when cheese is melted.

This is my family's favorite handmade pizza. You can make your own dough, like me, or you can find commercially made or boxed dough mixes at the grocery store. Lately I've noticed that some clubs are beginning to sell pizza dough by the case. There are lots of options. Just be sure to get enough dough to cover a 16-inch round or standard (15- by 10-inch) baking sheet. —KN

DAVE'S BARBECUED CHICKEN PIZZA

MAKES 6—8 SERVINGS

2 DAVE'S SWAMP BLUES BARBECUED CHICKEN HALF-BREASTS, GRILLED AND THINLY SLICED (PAGE 30)

1 pizza dough (about 24 ounces)

½ cup pizza sauce

1 tablespoon smoke-flavored barbecue sauce

3½ cups shredded mozzarella cheese (about 14 ounces)

½ cup shredded Cotija cheese (about 2 ounces)

1. Preheat the oven to 400°F.

2. Roll dough to the desired shape and size. Mix pizza sauce and barbecue sauce in a small bowl; spread over dough. Discard remaining sauce.

3. Spread mozzarella over sauce; top with chicken and sprinkle over shredded Cotija.

4. Bake pizza for 15 to 18 minutes, or until crust is golden brown and mozzarella is melted.

COTIJA CHEESE

Often compared to feta cheese because of its tangy flavor, Cotija is a common ingredient in Mexican cooking. It is available at Latino markets and more and more at grocery stores. Call first to check for availability before making a special trip. You're likely to find it near the deli in the specialty cheese case.

This recipe, another collaborative creation of ours, is simply outstanding. These rolls are perfect as a main dish on their own or as a potluck contribution. To feed a crowd, cut each piece of chicken into four smaller pieces after cooking. At home, complement the dish with a fresh citrus-jicama fruit salad. —KN / LT

MARIACHI CHICKEN ROLLS

MAKES 3 ENTRÉES, 4 SERVINGS EACH

1 TRAY (ABOUT 6 POUNDS) BONELESS, SKINLESS CHICKEN HALF-BREASTS

1 large red bell pepper, diced

4 scallions, chopped

1 (2¼-ounce) can chopped black olives (about ½ cup)

3 (8-ounce) packages light cream cheese, cubed and softened

3 cups prepared salsa

Paprika

Three 8-inch square baking dishes, greased

Plastic wrap

Aluminum foil

1. Combine pepper, scallions, and black olives in a small bowl. Set aside.

2. Blend cream cheese and salsa in a large bowl with an electric mixer. Set aside.

3. Rinse and trim chicken as desired. Slightly flatten the chicken by laying each piece, smooth side down, on a cutting board, and using the palm of your hand to press down on the thickest part of the chicken. Place 2 tablespoons of the pepper mixture near the wide end of each piece of chicken. Starting with the widest part of the breast, roll the chicken around the filling. Repeat with remaining chicken pieces. Divide rolls among the three baking dishes.

4. Divide cream cheese mixture evenly over each dish of chicken. Sprinkle with paprika to taste.

5. Wrap each dish entirely in plastic wrap. Top with foil, label, and freeze.

TO COOK ONE ENTRÉE

1. Completely thaw one entrée in the refrigerator.

2. Preheat the oven to 350°F.

3. Remove foil and plastic wrap from dish and replace foil. Bake, covered, for 1 hour, or until an instant-read thermometer inserted into the center of a roll reads 170°F.

FLASH FREEZING TIPS

To save space in the freezer and free up your dishes, consider flash freezing. This method allows you to individually freeze the rolls and store them in freezer bags instead of in the baking dishes. To flash freeze, evenly space rolls on a rimmed baking sheet and freeze. When the rolls are frozen solid, remove them from the freezer and divide them evenly among three labeled 1-gallon freezer bags. Divide the cream cheese mixture evenly among three 1-quart freezer bags. Place one bag of cream cheese mixture inside each bag of chicken. Seal and freeze. When it's time to cook, place the frozen chicken in a greased baking dish and thaw in the refrigerator. Thaw the cream cheese mixture in the refrigerator as well. When the cheese mixture has thawed, pour it over the rolls, top with paprika, and bake as directed.

This is a recipe that Lindsay and I worked on together. It was fun to test our new concoction and get rave reviews. Of all the dishes I cook, this is my mother-in-law's favorite. When I recently asked her what she might like for Christmas, she suggested that I make this recipe and leave the entrées in the freezer for her. I ended up leaving this and a dozen more. She was absolutely thrilled! Top this curry with any of the accompaniments listed on page 27. —KN / LT

MANGO-CRANBERRY CHICKEN

MAKES 4 ENTRÉES, 4 SERVINGS EACH

1 TRAY (ABOUT 6 POUNDS) BONELESS, SKINLESS CHICKEN HALF-BREASTS

½ cup chopped dried mango (about 4 ounces)

¼ cup dried cranberries

⅔ cup boiling water

2 (9-ounce) jars mango chutney (about 2 cups)

½ cup rice vinegar

¼ cup minced onion

1 tablespoon minced garlic (about 9 cloves)

1 tablespoon toasted sesame oil

1 tablespoon curry powder

4 one-gallon freezer bags, labeled

1. Rinse and trim chicken and cut into bite-size strips. Divide the chicken evenly among the four 1-gallon freezer bags.

2. Place mango and cranberries in a medium bowl and cover with boiling water; stir. Add chutney, vinegar, onion, garlic, sesame oil, and curry powder; stir. Divide cooled sauce evenly over the chicken.

3. Seal and freeze.

TO COOK ONE ENTRÉE

1. Completely thaw one entrée in the refrigerator.

2. Simmer chicken and sauce in a large skillet over medium heat until meat is thoroughly cooked, 15 to 20 minutes.

3. Serve hot over rice or noodles.

This dish retains the distinctive flavor of the liquor after it is cooked. If you prefer more subtle flavors, consider cutting the rum in half. I serve this with a fruit salad featuring red grapes, pineapple, mango, or peaches. —KN

MOLASSES-RUM CHICKEN

MAKES 3 ENTRÉES, 4 SERVINGS EACH

1 TRAY (ABOUT 6 POUNDS) BONELESS, SKINLESS CHICKEN HALF-BREASTS

1½ cups blackstrap rum (such as Cruzan), or other dark rum

¾ cup prepared barbecue sauce

⅔ cup lime juice

3 tablespoons molasses

3 tablespoons hot pepper sauce

2 tablespoons vegetable oil

1 tablespoon salt

3 one-gallon freezer bags, labeled

1. Rinse and trim chicken as desired. Divide chicken evenly among the three freezer bags.

2. Combine rum, barbecue sauce, lime juice, molasses, hot pepper sauce, oil, and salt in a large bowl. Divide the marinade evenly over the chicken.

3. Seal and freeze.

TO COOK ONE ENTRÉE

1. Completely thaw one entrée in the refrigerator.

2. Prepare a medium-low fire in a gas or charcoal grill.

3. Grill chicken, turning occasionally, for 30 minutes, or until an instant-read thermometer inserted into the thickest part of the chicken reads 170°F. Discard remaining marinade.

Here's a wonderful family-friendly recipe from our friend Shawnee, who told us: "My youngest loves those well-known fast food chicken bites. Looking for a healthier alternative, I combined and adapted several recipes to come up with a baked variation that the whole family enjoys." Try any leftover chicken strips chopped and served over salad with candied pecans, blue cheese, and honey mustard dressing. —KN / LT

PECAN-CRUSTED CHICKEN STRIPS

MAKES 3 ENTRÉES, ABOUT 12 STRIPS EACH

1 TRAY (ABOUT 6 POUNDS) BONELESS, SKINLESS CHICKEN HALF-BREASTS

2 cups honey

1 cup spicy brown mustard

¾ cup olive oil

1 tablespoon salt

1 tablespoon granulated garlic

1 tablespoon black pepper

3 cups panko (Japanese breadcrumbs)

1½ cups (8 ounces) pecans, finely ground

6 one-gallon freezer bags, label 3

3 one-quart freezer bags

1. Rinse and trim chicken as desired. Cut each half-breast lengthwise into three strips. Divide chicken evenly among the three unlabeled 1-gallon freezer bags.

2. Combine honey, mustard, oil, salt, garlic, and pepper in a medium bowl. Divide sauce evenly over the chicken.

3. Seal bags.

4. Into each of the three 1-quart freezer bags, measure 1 cup panko and ½ cup pecans; seal. Place one bag of chicken and one bag of pecan/breadcrumb mixture into each labeled 1-gallon bag.

5. Seal and freeze.

TO COOK ONE ENTRÉE

1. Completely thaw one entrée in the refrigerator.

2. Preheat the oven to 350°F.

3. Place breadcrumb mixture on a plate. Shake excess sauce off each piece of chicken, roll in crumbs, and place on a greased baking sheet.

4. Bake for 30 minutes, or until chicken pulls apart easily and is no longer pink in the thickest part, and crust is golden.

DOUBLE THE SAVINGS

Once you get the hang of our Tray Pack Method, you can begin making groups of recipes that use similar ingredients. This will allow you to take advantage of warehouse club pricing while also reducing waste.

Take honey as an example. Purchasing honey at the grocery store can cost 2 to 4 times more per ounce than at the warehouse club. Yet, to get that great price, you must buy a great amount — 96 ounces (6 pounds) at our local club versus 32 ounces (2 pounds) at the grocery store. Instead of passing up the value or having most of the bottle go unused, why not select several recipes that use large amounts of honey? The 8 cups of honey in that 96-ounce container can be used in one cooking session to make Pecan–Crusted Chicken Strips, Honey–Glazed Chicken Thighs, Honey and Spice Pork Kabobs, and Granola. Together, these recipes use 7 of the 8 cups in the large container, leaving a reasonable bit for day-to-day use.

The delicious handmade barbecue sauce in this dish, featuring port, offers more complex flavors than most other barbecue sauces. Feel free to pump up the zip by adding more crushed red pepper. Try this chicken in our Port BBQ Sauce Chicken Salad and on our Port BBQ Sauce Chicken Pizza on the following two pages. —KN

PORT BARBECUED CHICKEN

MAKES 3 ENTRÉES, 4 SERVINGS EACH

1 TRAY (ABOUT 6 POUNDS) BONELESS, SKINLESS CHICKEN HALF-BREASTS

½ cup (1 stick) butter

5 ounces shallots, minced (about 1 cup)

1½ tablespoons dry mustard

1½ teaspoons crushed red pepper flakes

2 cups ketchup

¾ cup Worcestershire sauce

⅓ cup port

⅓ cup water

½ cup packed dark brown sugar

¼ cup soy sauce

1 tablespoon molasses

3 one-gallon freezer bags, labeled

1. Melt butter in a large saucepan over medium heat. Add shallots; cook, stirring, 5 minutes. Add dry mustard and crushed red pepper; cook, stirring, 2 minutes longer, or until shallots are tender. Add ketchup, Worcestershire sauce, port, water, brown sugar, soy sauce, and molasses. Bring to a boil; reduce heat and simmer, stirring frequently, 20 minutes. Cool sauce.

2. While sauce is cooling, rinse and trim chicken as desired. Divide chicken evenly among the three freezer bags.

3. Divide cooled sauce evenly over the chicken.

4. Seal and freeze.

TO COOK ONE ENTRÉE

1. Completely thaw one entrée in the refrigerator.

2. Prepare a medium-low fire in a gas or charcoal grill.

3. Cook chicken, turning every 5 minutes and basting frequently with the marinade, for 30 minutes, or until an instant-read thermometer inserted into the thickest part of the chicken reads 170°F. Do not baste chicken during last 5 minutes of grilling.

4. Boil remaining sauce for at least 5 minutes if you wish to serve it with the chicken.

SHALLOTS

You can find shallots near the onions and garlic in your grocery store's produce section. Some people find the flavor of shallots to be a cross between a mild, sweet onion and garlic. Minced shallots will also add wonderful flavor to your favorite vinaigrette.

When I lived in the Seattle area, I wasted no time in trying all kinds of new restaurants and pubs. I came across a barbecued-chicken salad at one local restaurant that kept me coming back. I created this recipe to mimic the flavors in that memorable dish. —KN

CHICKEN SALAD
WITH PORT BARBECUE SAUCE

MAKES 4 SERVINGS

2 PORT BARBECUE CHICKEN IN SAUCE HALF-BREASTS, GRILLED AND THINLY SLICED (PAGE 40)

2 large hearts of romaine lettuce, rinsed and torn into bite-size pieces

1 cup black beans, rinsed and drained

1 cup frozen roasted corn

1 onion, sliced and caramelized (see note)

2 Roma tomatoes, quartered lengthwise

1 avocado, pitted, peeled, and cut into 8 wedges

½ cup ranch dressing

½ cup honey barbecue sauce

1. Place ¼ of the lettuce on each of four plates. Top lettuce with ¼ cup black beans, ¼ cup corn, ¼ of the chicken, ¼ of the onion, 2 tomato slices, and 2 avocado wedges.

2. Set out ranch dressing and barbecue sauce, allowing each person to use and combine dressings as desired. You may wish to thin the ranch a bit with water so that it pours easily and can be combined with the barbecue sauce.

CARAMELIZED ONIONS

To make caramelized onions, thinly slice an onion cut in half. Melt one tablespoon butter in a small skillet over medium-low heat. Brown onion strings slowly in butter, stirring occasionally, for 20 minutes. Stir in ½ teaspoon honey and cook an additional 5 minutes. The finished onions add a wonderful touch of sweetness and texture to salads, pizzas, and vegetables.

Every so often, we allow our kids to invite friends over for pizza and movie night. I always invite the parents to come, too. Recently we parents were having such a good time together we actually got shushed by the kids! I usually make three pizzas on these nights: cheese, olive, and either Port Barbecue Sauce Chicken or Dave's Barbecued Chicken Pizza (page 33). This port-sauce pizza is so good that the extra calories of a pizza dinner are worth the splurge. —KN

CHICKEN PIZZA
WITH PORT BARBECUE SAUCE

MAKES 6–8 SERVINGS

2 PORT BARBECUE CHICKEN IN SAUCE HALF-BREASTS, GRILLED AND THINLY SLICED (PAGE 40)

1 pizza dough (about 24 ounces)

½ cup pizza sauce

1 tablespoon honey barbecue sauce

3½ cups shredded mozzarella cheese (about 14 ounces)

½ cup shredded Asiago cheese

1. Preheat the oven to 400°F.

2. Roll dough to the desired shape and size. Mix pizza sauce and barbecue sauce in a small bowl; spread over dough.

3. Spread mozzarella over sauce; top with chicken and sprinkle over shredded Asiago.

4. Bake pizza for 15 to 18 minutes, or until crust is golden brown and mozzarella is melted.

As a practical, everyday cook, I usually don't bother with fancy food. But if I'm expecting special dinner guests, these rolls are great to have on hand. Since they are flash frozen, I can make up a batch and then pull them out a day or so before my event as the RSVPs roll in. —KN

CHICKEN ROLLS
WITH CRISPY ALMOND/RYE BREADING

MAKES 3 ENTRÉES, 4 SERVINGS EACH

1 TRAY (ABOUT 6 POUNDS) BONELESS, SKINLESS CHICKEN HALF-BREASTS

12 rye crispbread (such as Wasa) crackers, ground into crumbs, (See Note)

¾ cup smoked almonds, finely ground

3 egg whites, lightly beaten

1 (8-ounce) package cream cheese

Wax paper

12–14 toothpicks

6 one-gallon freezer bags, double bagged, label 3

NOTE: Use a food processor to finely grind rye crispbreads and smoked almonds.

1. Rinse and trim chicken as desired. Lay out two shallow dishes. Combine rye crispbread crumbs and ground almonds in one dish. To keep breading from absorbing excess moisture from the eggs, pour half the breading mixture into a small bowl and set aside; use this to refill the shallow breading dish as it empties. Put the egg whites in the second dish.

2. Working with 4 to 6 half-breasts at a time, lay each piece of chicken, smooth side down, between two sheets of wax paper. Pound chicken to ½-inch thickness with a rolling pin or meat tenderizer. Note the number of chicken pieces. Set chicken aside.

3. Slice the block of cream cheese lengthwise into two long strips, then cut the strips into cubes equal to the number of chicken half-breasts.

4. Spread one cream cheese cube on each piece of chicken. Starting from the widest end of each half-breast, roll the chicken and secure the end with a toothpick. Dip the chicken into the egg whites, then roll through the breadcrumb mixture until well covered. Place each chicken roll on a rimmed baking sheet. Discard remaining egg and breading.

5. Place coated chicken rolls in freezer for 1 hour. Divide frozen rolls evenly among the double-bagged freezer bags. Seal and return to freezer.

TO COOK ONE ENTRÉE

1. Remove rolls from freezer and place in a greased 9-inch square baking dish. Cover and place in the refrigerator to thaw completely.

2. Preheat the oven to 350°F.

3. Bake, uncovered, for 45 to 60 minutes, or until an instant-read thermometer inserted into the thickest part of a roll reads 170°F.

CHEESE FILLING

Cream cheese is a mild filling that appeals to many. More adventurous cooks can try different types of cheese. The cheese sections of the warehouse clubs are always expanding to include new varieties and flavors. A little gorgonzola mixed into the cream cheese? Boursin brand spreadable cheese? Feel free to experiment!

This recipe is based on several recipes and is the culmination of years of experimentation. At the time I created it, my husband's aunt was lending me copies of *Bon Appetit* and *Gourmet* magazines. This was in the pre-children phase of my life, when I had the time to read *Home Cooking* and *Sunset* also. My inspiration likely came from these sources, and was cultivated through years of feedback from my family. Children particularly enjoy the sweet Asian flavors of this marinated chicken breast. —KN

SWEET ASIAN CHICKEN

MAKES 3 ENTRÉES, 4 SERVINGS EACH

1 TRAY (ABOUT 6 POUNDS) BONELESS, SKINLESS CHICKEN HALF-BREASTS

1 cup packed brown sugar

1 cup soy sauce

¼ cup lime juice

½ teaspoon curry powder

3 tablespoons minced garlic (about 25 cloves)

2¼ teaspoons crushed red pepper flakes

3 one-gallon freezer bags, labeled

ON HAND FOR COOKING EACH ENTRÉE INDOORS

2 teaspoons peanut oil

1. Rinse and trim chicken as desired. Divide chicken evenly among the three freezer bags.

2. Combine the brown sugar, soy sauce, lime juice, and curry powder in a medium bowl. Divide marinade evenly over the chicken.

3. Measure 1 tablespoon minced garlic and ¾ teaspoon crushed red pepper into each bag.

4. Seal and freeze.

TO COOK ONE ENTRÉE

This entrée can be prepared outdoors on a grill or in the kitchen on your stovetop.

1. Completely thaw one entrée in the refrigerator.

FOR OUTDOOR COOKING

1. Prepare a medium-low fire in a gas or charcoal grill.

2. Cook chicken, turning every 5 minutes and basting frequently with the marinade, for 30 minutes, or until an instant-read thermometer inserted into the thickest part of the chicken reads 170°F. Do not baste chicken during last 5 minutes of grilling. Discard remaining marinade.

FOR INDOOR COOKING

Cut marinated chicken into ½-inch strips. Heat the oil in a wok or large skillet. Stir-fry chicken over medium heat for about 25 minutes, or until pieces pull apart easily and are no longer pink in the center. Serve with soba noodles or rice and sweet Asian coleslaw.

ABOUT MIXING MARINADES

In this recipe and in many others in the book, we ask you to divide the marinade evenly over the meat in the bags. Then, in a second step, you measure other ingredients, such as minced garlic, directly into each bag. We have found that certain ingredients will either sink to the bottom or float on top of a thin marinade, resulting in uneven distribution when the mixture is poured into the bags of meat. After you have all the ingredients in each bag, seal it and gently shake to combine its contents.

I developed this recipe after I noticed that an entrée by this name was a favorite restaurant choice of several of my girlfriends. If your dinner guests aren't familiar with this popular Thai dish, describe it as chicken in a spicy coconut milk sauce, served over fresh spinach and rice. —LT

SWIMMING RAMA

MAKES 3 ENTRÉES, 4—6 SERVINGS EACH

1 TRAY (ABOUT 6 POUNDS) BONELESS, SKINLESS CHICKEN HALF-BREASTS

3 (14-ounce) cans coconut milk

¼ cup fish sauce

2 tablespoons red curry paste

1 tablespoon honey

1½ cups dry-roasted unsalted peanuts, finely ground

3 one-gallon freezer bags, labeled

ON HAND FOR COOKING EACH ENTRÉE

Fresh spinach leaves

Steamed rice

1. Rinse and trim chicken as desired. Cut chicken into bite-size pieces.

2. Combine coconut milk, fish sauce, curry paste, and honey in a large skillet and bring to a simmer over medium heat. Add chicken and cook until no longer pink, about 20 minutes. Stir in ground peanuts. Remove from heat and cool.

3. Divide cooled chicken and sauce evenly among freezer bags.

4. Seal and freeze.

TO COOK ONE ENTRÉE

1. Completely thaw one entrée in the refrigerator.

2. In a large skillet over medium heat, bring the chicken and sauce to a simmer and cook until heated through. Do not boil.

3. To serve, place a handful of fresh spinach leaves on each person's plate. Top with a generous serving of chicken and sauce. Pass hot steamed rice at the table.

Don't let the cayenne scare you away from these tasty chicken fingers. They're great for lunch, dinner on the run, or as a party appetizer. Try dipping them in commercial salsa ranch dressing or chipotle barbecue sauce. Or slice the cooked fingers and serve atop salad or in wraps with black beans and other ingredients. —KN

TEX-MEX CHICKEN FINGERS

MAKES 3 ENTRÉES, ABOUT 12 FINGERS EACH

1 TRAY (ABOUT 6 POUNDS) BONELESS, SKINLESS CHICKEN HALF-BREASTS

4 eggs, lightly beaten

6 cups plain dry bread crumbs

3 tablespoons ground cumin

3 tablespoons granulated garlic

2 tablespoons chili powder

1 tablespoon salt

1 tablespoon cayenne pepper

Plastic wrap

3 one-gallon freezer bags, labeled

1. Rinse and trim chicken as desired. Cut each half-breast lengthwise into three strips. Set aside.

2. Place eggs in a shallow dish.

3. Combine breadcrumbs, cumin, garlic, chili powder, salt, and cayenne in a large bowl.

4. Dip each piece of chicken first into the egg and then into the breadcrumb mixture. Place breaded chicken pieces onto one or more baking sheets. Cover with plastic wrap and freeze until solid.

5. Once the chicken fingers are frozen, remove from baking sheets and divide evenly among the 1-gallon freezer bags. Seal and return to the freezer.

TO COOK ONE ENTRÉE

1. Completely thaw one entrée in the refrigerator.

2. Preheat the oven to 350°F.

3. Bake chicken fingers on a greased baking sheet for 30 minutes, or until chicken pulls apart easily and is no longer pink in the center of the thickest portion.

The first time I tested this recipe on my family, my six-year-old enjoyed the dish so much, she ate an entire half-breast herself — and asked for seconds. It has since become a family favorite. My cousin Taryn enjoys using the leftover chicken in taco salads with the works: avocado, fresh cherry tomatoes, fresh salsa, and a sprinkling of Cotija cheese. —KN

TEQUILA-LIME CHICKEN

MAKES 3 ENTRÉES, 4 SERVINGS EACH

1 TRAY (ABOUT 6 POUNDS) BONELESS, SKINLESS CHICKEN HALF-BREASTS

¾ cup soy sauce

½ cup bottled margarita mix

3 tablespoons tequila

3 tablespoons lime juice

1 tablespoon dry mustard

3 teaspoons minced garlic (about 9 cloves)

3 one-gallon freezer bags, labeled

1. Rinse and trim chicken as desired. Divide chicken evenly among the freezer bags.

2. Combine soy sauce, margarita mix, tequila, lime juice, and mustard in a medium bowl. Divide marinade evenly over the chicken. Into each bag measure 1 teaspoon minced garlic.

3. Seal and freeze.

TO COOK ONE ENTRÉE

This entrée can be prepared outdoors on a grill or in the kitchen using your broiler.

1. Completely thaw one entrée in the refrigerator.

TEQUILA TIP

Those large bottles of tequila can be costly. If this recipe is the only reason to have tequila on hand, look for the tiny 50-mL bottle at your liquor store. You'll find you have enough for this recipe with a few drops left over.

FOR OUTDOOR COOKING

1. Prepare a medium-low fire in a gas or charcoal grill.

2. Cook chicken, turning every 5 minutes and basting frequently with the marinade, for 30 minutes, or until an instant-read thermometer inserted into the thickest part of the chicken reads 170°F. Do not baste chicken during last 5 minutes of grilling. Discard remaining marinade.

FOR INDOOR COOKING

Slice each breast in half horizontally, so that no piece is more than 1 inch thick. Arrange the chicken slices on a greased broiler pan. Broil chicken 5 inches from the broiler, turning frequently and basting, for 15 to 20 minutes, or until an instant-read thermometer inserted into the thickest part of the chicken reads 170°F. Do not baste chicken during last 5 minutes of grilling. Discard remaining marinade.

Another delicious recipe from our friend Shawnee. She says, "Cashews are such a delicious addition to a dish. Technically not a nut but a seed, cashews dare you to eat just a few. They actually have a lower fat content than almonds, walnuts, pecans, and peanuts, and are packed with nutrients." —KN / LT

CASHEW CHICKEN STIR-FRY

MAKES 3 ENTRÉES, 4–6 SERVINGS EACH

1 TRAY (ABOUT 6 POUNDS) BONELESS, SKINLESS CHICKEN THIGHS

¾ cup soy sauce

⅓ cup red wine or cooking sherry

1 tablespoon fish sauce

3 teaspoons minced garlic (about 9 cloves)

2¼ teaspoons minced ginger

1½ teaspoons crushed red pepper flakes

3 cups unsalted cashews

6 one-gallon freezer bags, label 3

3 sandwich bags

ON HAND FOR COOKING EACH ENTRÉE

½ pound assorted fresh vegetables, cut into 1-inch pieces for stir-frying

2 teaspoons sesame oil

1. Rinse chicken and cut into bite-size pieces. Divide the chicken evenly among the three unlabeled 1-gallon freezer bags.

2. Combine the soy sauce, wine, and fish sauce in a medium bowl. Divide marinade evenly over the chicken. Into each bag measure 1 teaspoon garlic, ¾ teaspoon ginger, and ½ teaspoon crushed red pepper. Seal bags.

3. Put 1 cup cashews into each of the sandwich bags and seal.

4. Place a bag of chicken and a bag of cashews into each of the labeled 1-gallon bags. Seal and freeze.

TO COOK ONE ENTRÉE

1. Completely thaw one entrée in the refrigerator.

2. Heat sesame oil in a wok or large skillet. Stir-fry chicken and sauce over medium-high heat until meat is cooked through, 20 to 25 minutes. Remove chicken from the pan.

3. Add vegetables and stir-fry until tender crisp, about 5 minutes. Return chicken to pan and stir to combine. Sprinkle with cashews and serve.

WHERE'S THE FISH SAUCE?

Fish sauce, a condiment used in Southeast Asian cuisine, adds depth to marinades and stir-fry sauces. Look for it in the Asian aisle at your super-market. There you'll also find toasted sesame oil, hoisin sauce, mango chutney, coconut milk, and red curry paste, which are called for in several other recipes.

These kabobs make a delightful alternative to the usual fare, and they're easy to prepare year round. If you plan to use disposable wooden skewers, remember to soak them in water before threading on the chicken. Whether grilled or broiled, the kabobs pair well with sticky white rice and steamed fresh vegetables. —KN / LT

PEANUT SATAY

MAKES 3 ENTRÉES, 4–6 SERVINGS EACH

1 TRAY (ABOUT 6 POUNDS) BONELESS, SKINLESS CHICKEN THIGHS

¾ cup natural chunky peanut butter

½ cup orange juice concentrate, thawed

⅓ cup soy sauce

1 tablespoon minced ginger

2 teaspoons orange zest

½ teaspoon hot pepper sauce

5 scallions, chopped (about ¾ cup)

3 one-gallon freezer bags, labeled

ON HAND FOR COOKING EACH ENTRÉE

8 (9-inch) wooden or metal skewers

1. Rinse chicken and cut into ½ inch strips. Divide chicken evenly among the three 1-gallon bags.

2. Combine peanut butter, juice concentrate, soy sauce, ginger, orange zest, and hot pepper sauce in a medium bowl; divide evenly over the chicken. Into each bag measure about ¼ cup scallions.

3. Seal and gently shake bag to distribute scallions. Freeze.

WHAT IS ZEST?

When a recipe calls for the zest of a citrus fruit, it's referring to the colorful part of the skin. Don't confuse the zest with the white pith part, between the fruit and zest, as it can be quite bitter. To remove the zest, wash and dry the fruit. Then, using a zester or fine grater, gently shave the colorful, outermost part of the peel.

TO COOK ONE ENTRÉE

This entrée can be prepared outdoors on a grill or in the kitchen using your broiler.

1. Completely thaw one entrée in the refrigerator.

FOR OUTDOOR COOKING

1. Prepare a medium-low fire in a gas or charcoal grill.

2. If using wooden skewers, soak them in water while chicken is thawing. Thread chicken pieces onto skewers. Grill until chicken pulls apart easily and is no longer pink in the center of the thickest portion. Discard remaining marinade.

FOR INDOOR COOKING

Thread chicken pieces onto skewers. Arrange the kabobs on a greased broiler pan. Broil chicken 5 inches from the heat for 10 to 14 minutes, turning frequently, until chicken pulls apart easily and is no longer pink in the center of the thickest portion. Discard remaining marinade.

LITE SOY SAUCE

If you're watching your sodium intake, consider using "lite" or "lower sodium" soy sauce. It's readily available in grocery stores next to the regular soy sauce.

You'll be amazed that the simple ingredients in this dish can produce such a delicious meal. When I ask my children what they want for dinner, this is often their request. Sure to be a hit in your house, too, it goes straight from the freezer to the oven. Easy on the cook! —LT

HONEY-GLAZED CHICKEN THIGHS

MAKES 3 ENTRÉES, 4 SERVINGS EACH

1 TRAY (ABOUT 7 POUNDS, OR 16 PIECES) CHICKEN THIGHS ON THE BONE, SKIN REMOVED

1½ cups honey

¾ cup butter (do not substitute margarine)

½ cup prepared mustard

1 tablespoon curry powder

2 teaspoons salt

3 one-gallon freezer bags, labeled

1. Combine honey, butter, mustard, curry powder, and salt in a medium saucepan. Cook, stirring, over medium heat until all the ingredients dissolve into a smooth sauce, about 3 minutes. Cool.

2. While sauce is cooling, rinse and divide chicken evenly among freezer bags. Divide cooled sauce evenly over the chicken.

3. Seal and freeze.

TO COOK ONE ENTRÉE

1. Thaw one entrée in the refrigerator just long enough to remove from the freezer bag.

2. Preheat the oven to 350°F.

3. Place frozen chicken in an ungreased baking dish. Bake for 45 minutes. Remove dish from oven and separate chicken pieces into a single layer, placing pieces meaty side down to keep them moist. Bake for 1½ hours longer, or until the sauce has browned and is thick and sticky. The chicken will be thoroughly cooked but still moist from the sauce.

FREEZE FIRST!

Most of our recipes are equally good if cooked and eaten the same day they are prepared or frozen first. A few should be frozen before cooking. This recipe should be frozen and baked unthawed to allow the sauce time to caramelize before the chicken becomes overcooked.

In the first few years of my marriage, there were several people I could rely on to provide me with excellent recipes. Two such friends were Debbie and Terry, sisters who are both excellent cooks. They have generously shared their best recipe finds with me over the years, and this is my version of one of those gems. The recipe was not one of our original picks for this book, but it made the cut after several people begged us to include it. —LT

ROYAL THAI THIGHS

MAKES 3 ENTRÉES, 4 SERVINGS EACH

1 TRAY (ABOUT 7 POUNDS, OR 16 PIECES) CHICKEN THIGHS ON THE BONE, SKIN REMOVED

6 scallions, chopped

¾ cup hoisin sauce

½ cup natural peanut butter

½ cup water

¼ cup soy sauce

¼ cup toasted sesame oil

¼ cup lemon juice

6 teaspoons minced garlic

6 teaspoons minced ginger

1½ teaspoons crushed red pepper flakes (optional)

3 one-gallon freezer bags, labeled

1. Rinse and divide chicken evenly among freezer bags.

2. Whisk together scallions, hoisin, peanut butter, water, soy sauce, sesame oil, and lemon juice in a medium bowl; divide the sauce evenly over the chicken. Into each bag measure 2 teaspoons garlic and 2 teaspoons ginger. Add ½ teaspoon crushed red pepper to each bag, if desired.

3. Seal and freeze.

TO COOK ONE ENTRÉE

1. Completely thaw one entrée in the refrigerator.

2. Preheat the oven to 375°F.

3. Place chicken in a lightly greased baking dish. Bake, uncovered, for 45 minutes, or until an instant-read thermometer inserted into the thickest part of the chicken reads 180°F.

HEAT UNITS

Hot peppers can be classified according to their Scoville heat units. The range of heat among peppers is large, with green bell peppers having 0 heat units and habaneros registering a sizzling 300,000 units or more. Thai food lovers and other food adventurers can substitute a hotter pepper for the crushed red pepper (approximately 20,000 heat units) in this recipe. Traditional Thai peppers, also called Asian hot, Thai hot, or bird peppers, can measure up to 100,000 heat units.

The simple sauce for this dish is always a hit with kids. You can substitute chicken legs for the thighs in this recipe. Or, if you prefer a stir-fry, marinate strips of chicken breast in the sauce, then stir-fry in a very hot pan with a little oil. —LT

TERIYAKI CHICKEN

MAKES 3 ENTRÉES, 4 SERVINGS EACH

1 TRAY (ABOUT 7 POUNDS, OR 16 PIECES) CHICKEN THIGHS ON THE BONE, SKIN REMOVED

1 cup soy sauce

1 cup packed brown sugar

¼ cup red wine vinegar

1 tablespoon vegetable oil

3 teaspoons minced garlic (about 9 cloves)

3 teaspoons minced ginger

3 one-gallon freezer bags, labeled

1. Rinse and divide chicken evenly among freezer bags.

2. Combine, stirring until sugar is dissolved, soy sauce, brown sugar, vinegar, and oil in a small bowl. Divide the marinade evenly over the chicken. Into each bag measure 1 teaspoon garlic and 1 teaspoon ginger.

3. Seal and freeze.

TO COOK ONE ENTRÉE

1. Completely thaw one entrée in the refrigerator.

2. Preheat the oven to 350°F.

3. Place chicken in an ungreased baking dish. Bake, uncovered, for 1 hour, or until an instant-read thermometer inserted into the thickest part of the chicken reads 180°F. Turn pieces once or twice during baking. The longer the cooking time, the thicker and stickier the sauce will be.

This recipe comes from our friend and colleague Shawnee. Here's what she says about her creation: "A dish so simple, it seems like no work at all. The combination of flavors came to me when I noticed both frozen mixed berries and berry salad dressing on a visit to my favorite warehouse store. My mother-in-law used to encourage me to pop a whole chicken into the oven when I got home from work, but I never did that until I created this easy recipe that has since become a staple in our household." —KN / LT

BERRY-ROASTED CHICKEN

MAKES 2 ENTRÉES, 4–6 SERVINGS EACH

1 TWO-PACK (8–10 POUNDS TOTAL WEIGHT) WHOLE CHICKENS

2 cups berry-flavored vinaigrette dressing (try our handmade version on page 186)

2 cups (12 ounces) frozen mixed berries

1 cup chopped onion (about 1 medium)

½ teaspoon salt

½ teaspoon black pepper

2 one-gallon freezer bags, labeled

ON HAND FOR COOKING EACH ENTRÉE

Fresh raspberries (optional)

1. Rinse chickens under cool running water. Remove neck and giblets from cavity and discard. Pat chickens dry with paper towel.

2. Put one chicken into each 1-gallon bag. Over each chicken, measure 1 cup vinaigrette, 1 cup berries, ½ cup onion, ¼ teaspoon salt, and ¼ teaspoon pepper.

3. Seal and freeze.

TO COOK ONE ENTRÉE

1. Completely thaw one bag of chicken in the refrigerator.

2. Preheat the oven to 325°F.

3. Place chicken, breast side up, in a greased baking dish and pour marinade into cavity. Roast for about 1½ hours, or until an instant-read thermometer inserted into the thigh reads 180°F. Garnish with fresh raspberries, if desired.

The sweet flavors in this dish are a twist on traditional southwestern cooking. This versatile filling can be used on regular tostada shells in place of ground beef or beans. You might also consider using it in our Cinco Layer Bake and Sweet Chicken Tostada Crowns on the following pages. —KN

SWEET CHICKEN TOSTADA FILLING

MAKES ABOUT 14½ CUPS

1 TWO-PACK (8–10 POUNDS TOTAL WEIGHT) WHOLE CHICKENS

3 (8-ounce) packages cream cheese, softened

3 cups prepared mango salsa (such as Santa Barbara)

5 one-quart freezer bags, *labeled*

1. Clean and cook both chickens (see Cooking Methods, page 65). Cool and pull meat from bones. Discard skin and bones. Cut chicken into bite-size pieces. (A whole chicken will yield about 1 cup of meat per pound.)

2. Beat together cream cheese and salsa in a large bowl with an electric mixer. Stir in chicken. Divide mixture evenly among freezer bags, about 3 scant cups of filling in each.

3. Seal and freeze.

TO COOK ONE ENTRÉE

1. Completely thaw one bag of filling in the refrigerator.

2. Bring the filling to a simmer in a large skillet over medium-low heat. Do not boil. Use as a filling for tacos, tostadas, or burritos.

You'll notice the ingredient list calls for Sweet Chicken Tostada Filling (page 61) and Chipotle Roasted-Tomato Sauce (page 176). Canned enchilada sauce works well, too, but we prefer it like this. Serve with a fresh green salad or fruit salad with jicama. —KN

CINCO LAYER BAKE

MAKES 6–8 SERVINGS

2¾ CUPS (1-QUART BAG) SWEET CHICKEN TOSTADA FILLING (PAGE 61), THAWED

6 ten-inch flour tortillas, cut in half

1½ cups black beans, rinsed and drained

1 cup Chipotle Roasted-Tomato Sauce (page 176)

2 cups shredded Mexican blend cheese

2 medium tomatoes, chopped (optional)

Vegetable cooking spray

Aluminum foil

1. Preheat the oven to 375°F.

2. Lightly coat the bottom of a 9-inch square baking dish with cooking spray. Cover the bottom entirely with 4 of the tortilla halves, overlapping as necessary. Spread 1½ cups of the tostada filling over tortillas. Next layer with ¾ cup of the beans, ½ cup of the tomato sauce, and 1 cup of the cheese. Repeat with a layer of tortillas and the remaining filling, beans, and tomato sauce. Add the remaining 4 tortilla halves and top with 1 cup cheese.

3. Cover with foil and bake for 45 to 60 minutes, or until an instant-read thermometer inserted into the center of the casserole reads 165°F.

4. Garnish with fresh tomatoes, guacamole, or salsa, if desired.

JUST RIGHT

Some people like their enchiladas gooey, whereas others prefer them drier and crunchy. Some like more black beans, others prefer less. Whatever your preferences, feel free to adjust the ingredients to your taste.

Tostada crowns, sometimes called tostada bowls because of their shape, offer a fun way to present a meal. The filling here is sweet and mild, but you can turn up the heat by mixing in jalapeños. Served for Cinco de Mayo or another festive occasion, these are sure to please. —KN

SWEET CHICKEN TOSTADA CROWNS

MAKES 4 SERVINGS

2 CUPS SWEET CHICKEN TOSTADA FILLING (PAGE 61), WARMED

4 tostada crowns

2 cups black beans, rinsed and drained

6 cups shredded lettuce

2 cups cooked brown rice, cooled

1⅓ cups shredded Mexican blend cheese

8 tablespoons prepared salsa, or more to taste

1 mango, peeled and chopped

OPTIONAL TOPPINGS

Salsa, guacamole, sliced black olives, chopped tomatoes, or chopped green or red bell peppers

1. Place one tostada crown on each of four plates. Spread ½ cup chicken filling on the bottom of each crown; then layer with ½ cup black beans, 1½ cups lettuce, ½ cup rice, ⅓ cup cheese, 2 tablespoons salsa, and ¼ of the mango pieces.

2. Pass additional toppings at the table, if desired.

My version of this popular dish is made from scratch and is something I like to pull out when only comfort food will do. This versatile dish is equally tasty over mashed potatoes, rice, noodles, or biscuits. —LT

CHICKEN À LA KING

MAKES 4 ENTRÉES, 6 SERVINGS EACH

1 TWO-PACK (8–10 POUNDS TOTAL WEIGHT) WHOLE CHICKENS

1 cup (2 sticks) butter

1 pound fresh white mushrooms, cleaned and sliced

1 cup all-purpose flour

6 cups half-and-half (or light cream)

3 cups water

2 tablespoons chicken bouillon granules

1 teaspoon black pepper

4 green bell peppers, cut into 1-inch pieces

4 one-gallon freezer bags, labeled

1. Clean and cook both chickens (see Cooking Methods, page 65).

2. Cool and pull meat from bones. Discard skin and bones. Cut chicken into bite-size pieces. (A whole chicken will yield about 1 cup of meat per pound.) Divide chicken evenly among freezer bags.

3. Melt butter in a large saucepan over medium heat. Add mushrooms; cook, stirring, until soft. Add flour; cook, stirring, for 2 minutes. Mixture will be lumpy. Gradually add half-and-half, then water, stirring constantly until sauce thickens. Whisk to make a smooth sauce. Stir in bouillon and black pepper. Cool sauce.

4. Divide cooled sauce evenly over the chicken. Divide bell peppers evenly among the bags of chicken.

5. Seal and freeze.

TO COOK ONE ENTRÉE

1. Completely thaw one entrée in the refrigerator.

2. Simmer the chicken and sauce in a large skillet over medium heat until warmed through. Do not boil.

TWO COOKING METHODS FOR WHOLE CHICKENS

We recommend you use one of two methods for cooking two whole chickens at once — slow cooking or oven roasting. You will need a 6-quart slow cooker or an oven roasting pan with a lid (or a deep pan and some foil to cover). It makes no difference what the chickens look like when they are cooked since you will be pulling them apart, so if you have to turn them any which way to fit them in the slow cooker or you decide to roast them breast side down to retain moisture in the white meat, you may do so. Each of these cooking methods has its advantages. Slow cooking produces a more flavorful broth while oven roasting is much faster.

SLOW COOKING

Rinse chickens under cool running water. Remove neck and giblets from cavity and discard. Place both chickens in a 6-quart slow cooker with one cup water and two bay leaves; cook on low for 8 to 10 hours, or overnight. Drain and reserve juices. Discard bay leaves. Refrigerate juices. Cool chicken until it is no longer too hot to handle. Pull meat from bones and cut it into bite-size pieces. Discard skin and bones. Remove fat from the top of the reserved chicken juices. Use the broth to replace the broth or bouillon in any of the chicken recipes.

OVEN ROASTING

Rinse chickens under cool running water. Remove neck and giblets from cavity and discard. Place both chickens in a large roasting pan with two cups water and two bay leaves; bake covered at 350°F for 2 hours. Drain and reserve juices. Discard bay leaves. Refrigerate juices. Cool chicken until it is no longer too hot to handle. Pull meat from bones and cut it into bite-size pieces. Discard skin and bones. Remove fat from the top of the reserved chicken juices. Use the broth to replace the broth or bouillon in any of the chicken recipes.

Our colleague Shawnee writes of her recipe: "If you're looking for a 'wow' meal, this is it. Inserting lemon slices under the breast skin turns the humble chicken into a feast for the eyes and the palate. Add a side dish of couscous with pine nuts, make a simple cucumber and yogurt salad, and spread a colorful cloth on the table — wow!" —KN / LT

MEDITERRANEAN ROAST CHICKEN

MAKES 2 ENTRÉES, 4–6 SERVINGS EACH

1 TWO-PACK (8–10 POUNDS TOTAL WEIGHT) WHOLE CHICKENS

2 lemons

1 (16-ounce) container pitted Kalamata olives (about 1 cup), drained

4 tablespoons capers, rinsed and drained

2 tablespoons olive oil

2 teaspoons minced garlic (about 6 cloves)

1 teaspoon black pepper

½ teaspoon salt

2 one-gallon freezer bags, labeled

1. Zest the rind of both lemons. Cut one lemon into thin slices.

2. Rinse chickens under cool running water. Remove neck and giblets from cavity and discard. Pat chickens dry with paper towels.

3. Place chickens, breast side up, on a work surface. Gently loosen breast skin by working your fingers between skin and meat. Slide lemon slices under breast skin of each chicken. Put one chicken into each 1-gallon bag.

4. Divide the lemon zest evenly over the chickens. Juice the remaining lemon. Remove seeds and divide the juice evenly over the chickens. Into each bag measure ½ cup olives, 2 tablespoons capers, 1 tablespoon oil, 1 teaspoon garlic, ½ teaspoon pepper, and ¼ teaspoon salt.

5. Seal and freeze.

TO COOK ONE ENTRÉE

1. Completely thaw one bag of chicken in the refrigerator.

2. Preheat the oven to 325°F.

3. Place the chicken, breast side up, in a greased baking dish. Surround chicken with olives, capers, and marinade. Add just enough water to cover the bottom of the baking dish. Roast for about 1½ hours, or until an instant-read thermometer inserted into the thigh reads 180°F.

JUICING LEMONS

In his book *What Einstein Told His Cook*, Robert Wolke recommends first rolling the fruit on the counter and then heating it for 20 to 30 seconds in the microwave. Try this method (but be careful, the lemon could get hot!) only if you're squeezing the fruit by hand. If using an electric juicer or reamer, don't bother. As Wolke notes, you won't get any extra juice out of the lemon by using his method, but it will make squeezing out the lemon juice easier.

Many warehouses sell large fresh and frozen chicken potpies. Individuals who are sensitive to salt may appreciate this alternative to store-bought versions. Kids will have fun using a cookie cutter to cut the bread circles. —KN

MINI CHICKEN POTPIE

MAKES 5–6 ENTRÉES, 12 MINI POTPIES EACH

1 TWO-PACK (8–10 POUNDS TOTAL WEIGHT) WHOLE CHICKENS

4 tablespoons butter

2 cups sliced carrots (about 5 medium)

½ cup diced onion

⅔ cup all-purpose flour

2 tablespoons poultry seasoning

2 teaspoons salt

3 cups chicken juices, reserved from cooked chickens and cooled

3 cups half-and-half (or light cream)

1 (10-ounce) package frozen peas (about 2½ cups)

6 one-quart freezer bags, labeled

ON HAND FOR COOKING EACH ENTRÉE

12 slices of sandwich bread, cut into 3½-inch circles

1. Clean and cook both chickens (see Cooking Methods, page 65).

2. Cool and pull meat from bones. Discard skin and bones. Reserve 3 cups chicken juices. Cut chicken into bite-size pieces. (A whole chicken will yield about 1 cup of meat per pound.)

3. Melt butter in a large stockpot. Add carrots and cook, stirring, for 7 minutes. Add onion; cook, stirring, for 3 minutes longer, or until vegetables are soft. Stir in flour, poultry seasoning, and salt. Gradually add reserved chicken juices and half-and-half; stir constantly until sauce thickens. Cool sauce.

4. Add chicken and peas to cooled sauce. Spoon 2½ cups of chicken filling into each 1-quart freezer bag.

5. Seal and freeze.

TO COOK ONE ENTRÉE

1. Completely thaw one bag of filling in the refrigerator.

2. Preheat the oven to 350°F.

3. Gently press bread rounds into a greased 12-cup regular muffin tin, so that the bottom and sides are covered. The bread may not go all the way to the top of each form. Toast bread in the oven 8 to 10 minutes, or to desired firmness and color.

4. While bread is toasting, bring the chicken filling to a simmer in a medium saucepan. Do not boil.

5. Remove toasted bread cups from muffin tin. Fill each bread cup with chicken filling and serve.

OTHER FILLINGS

In *The Big Book of Preserving the Harvest* (see resources, page 241), author Carol Costenbader provides recipes for appetizers using mini bread cups. Use her Bacon and Cheese Filling for brunch or the Shrimp and Cheese variation for that special evening event. Carol also recommends freezing the bread cups, which can be handy when you're planning for a dinner party. However, if you're short on freezer space, make them as directed above.

When I worried that this recipe was too high in fat, my husband said, "This is a celebration dish!" Save this recipe for special occasions, and you'll decide it's worth the extra calories. A huge platter of delicious enchiladas requiring virtually no work from you at mealtime is a perfect choice for entertaining. To cut down on the fat, try light sour cream, light cream cheese, and white sauce made with skim milk. —LT

PARTY ENCHILADAS

MAKES 3 ENTRÉES, 6 SERVINGS EACH

1 TWO-PACK (8–10 POUNDS TOTAL WEIGHT) WHOLE CHICKENS

2 (8-ounce) packages cream cheese, softened

3 cups sour cream

1 (4-ounce) can diced green chilies (about 6 tablespoons)

1 tablespoon minced garlic (about 9 cloves)

1 tablespoon lime juice

2 teaspoons salt

2 teaspoons black pepper

1 teaspoon chili powder

18 ten-inch flour tortillas

1 recipe Chicken White Sauce (recipe follows)

1 cup prepared salsa

3 cups shredded Cheddar cheese (about 12 ounces)

3 (2¼-ounce) cans sliced black olives (about 1½ cups)

Three 13- by 9-inch baking dishes

Plastic wrap

Aluminum foil

1. Clean and cook both chickens (see Cooking Methods, page 65).

2. Cool and pull meat from bones. Discard skin and bones. Cut chicken into bite-size pieces. (A whole chicken will yield about 1 cup of meat per pound.)

3. Beat cream cheese in a large bowl with an electric mixer until smooth. Blend in sour cream, chilies, garlic, lime juice, salt, pepper, and chili powder. Stir in cooked chicken pieces.

4. To make the enchiladas, lay the tortillas out on a large work surface and divide the filling evenly among them. The amount of filling in each will vary depending on how much meat came off the chickens. Roll tortillas, folding ends in so the enchiladas will fit in the dish. Place 6 filled tortillas in each baking dish.

5. Stir salsa into the prepared white sauce; divide evenly over the dishes of enchiladas. Sprinkle each dish with 1 cup cheese and ½ cup black olives. Wrap each dish entirely in plastic wrap. Top with foil, label, and freeze.

TO COOK ONE ENTRÉE

1. Completely thaw one dish in the refrigerator.

2. Remove plastic wrap and foil and replace foil.

3. Preheat the oven to 350°F.

4. Bake, covered, for 25 minutes. Remove foil and bake 5 to 10 minutes longer, or until sauce is bubbling.

CHICKEN WHITE SAUCE

MAKES 4 CUPS

This versatile sauce can also be used anywhere you would normally use condensed cream of chicken soup. If you prefer a thinner sauce, stir in milk or broth a couple tablespoons at a time until it reaches the desired consistency.

½ cup (1 stick) butter, ¾ cup all-purpose flour, 1 tablespoon chicken bouillon granules, 2 cups water, 2 cups half-and-half (or milk, if you prefer)

Melt butter in a medium saucepan over medium heat. Add flour and bouillon; stir into a paste. Cook, stirring, for 2 minutes. Gradually add water and half-and-half; cook, stirring constantly, until the sauce has thickened, about 8 minutes.

I have my sister Shannon to thank for the name of this dish. During a telephone conversation one day, I said "herb and garlic," which she heard as "urban garlic." It stuck. —LT

URBAN GARLIC CHICKEN

MAKES 2 ENTRÉES, 4–6 SERVINGS EACH

1 TWO-PACK (8–10 POUNDS TOTAL WEIGHT) WHOLE CHICKENS

¼ cup olive oil

2 tablespoons red wine vinegar

1 tablespoon minced garlic (about 9 cloves)

1 tablespoon dried thyme

2 teaspoons salt

1 teaspoon black pepper

2 carrots, peeled and cut in half

2 celery stalks, cut in half

1 onion, peeled and cut in half

2 one-gallon freezer bags, labeled

2 one-quart freezer bags

1. Rinse chickens under cool running water. Remove neck and giblets from cavity and discard. Pat chickens dry with paper towel.

2. Combine oil, vinegar, garlic, thyme, salt, and pepper in a small bowl.

3. Place chickens, breast side up, on a work surface. Gently loosen skin on breast and legs by working your fingers between skin and meat. Using half the marinade for each chicken, rub under and over the skin and in the cavity. Put one chicken in each 1-gallon bag.

4. Divide carrots, celery, and onion evenly between the 1-quart bags and seal. Place one bag of vegetables directly into each bag of chicken.

5. Seal and freeze.

TO COOK ONE ENTRÉE

1. Completely thaw one entrée in the refrigerator.

2. Preheat the oven to 325°F.

3. Place chicken, breast side up, in a greased baking dish. Put carrot, celery, and onion in cavity. Roast for about 1½ hours, or until an instant-read thermometer inserted into the thigh reads 180°F.

OR TRY THIS!

Instead of thawing the chicken to roast it, place the frozen prepared chicken and vegetables in the slow cooker. Do this only if you have a slow cooker with a removable insert. Cook on low for 8 to 10 hours. Drain juices, reserve, and cool. Place the uncovered crock in a 350°F oven for 15 minutes to brown the skin. Meanwhile, use the reserved juices to make gravy or a sauce reduction. This might be the most flavorful, moist chicken dinner you will ever eat! Not to mention the fabulous gravy . . .

CHAPTER TWO

BEEF MAIN DISHES

We keep these on hand for quick lunches — homemade "fast food." —LT

BEEF AND BEAN BURRITOS

MAKES 40 BURRITOS

**1 TRAY (ABOUT 6 POUNDS)
LEAN GROUND BEEF**

1 cup taco seasoning

3 cups water

40 ten-inch flour tortillas

8 (15-ounce) cans refried beans, any
variety

Aluminum foil

8 one-gallon freezer bags, labeled

1. Brown beef in a large stockpot over medium heat until
no longer pink, about 20 minutes. Drain and discard fat.
Add the taco seasoning. Stir in water and simmer mixture over medium heat for 20 minutes, or until the liquid
is almost entirely evaporated. Cool.

2. Spread ¼ cup ground beef and ⅓ cup refried beans
on each tortilla. Wrap burrito-style and then wrap each
piece individually in foil. Divide packets evenly among
freezer bags.

3. Seal and freeze.

TO COOK ONE ENTRÉE

Thaw the burritos in the refrigerator or reheat them
straight from the freezer.

MICROWAVE
Remove foil, defrost, and reheat.

OVEN
Bake in foil at 375°F for 30 minutes if frozen, 300°F for
30 minutes if thawed.

HOMEMADE REFRIED BEANS

You may prefer to make your own refried beans, as I do. To have the right amount for this recipe, begin with 2½ pounds (about 5 cups) of dried pinto beans. Put them in a large stockpot with plenty of water to cover. Bring the beans to a boil; boil for 2 minutes. Turn off the heat, cover the pot, and let the beans stand for 1 hour. Drain, rinse the beans, and return them to the pot. Add 15 cups water and simmer for 2 hours. At this point, authentic refried beans would be mashed with some of the cooking water and then fried in lard. I prefer to pulse the cooked beans to the desired consistency in my food processor and forego the frying altogether. Season the beans according to your preference — salt, pepper, garlic, cumin, and chili powder are nice choices. Because I use these beans with the seasoned beef in the burritos, I add just a bit of salt and pepper.

If ever there was a "football food," this qualifies. Our favorite football team is not on television every week, so I try to save this dish for the times when it is. The last thing I want to do is miss any part of the game, and this dish is great: I simply take it out of the oven and set out the chips, salsa, and drinks. Touchdown! —KN

CHEESY CHILADA BAKE

MAKES 4 ENTRÉES, 8 SERVINGS EACH

1 TRAY (ABOUT 6 POUNDS) LEAN GROUND BEEF

4 green bell peppers, diced

4 medium onions, diced

2 teaspoons minced garlic (about 6 cloves)

4 cups picante sauce

4 (15-ounce) cans tomato sauce

4 (14½-ounce) cans pinto beans

2 teaspoons ground cumin

2 teaspoons salt

48 corn tortillas

8 cups shredded Mexican cheese blend (about 2 pounds)

4 13- by 9-inch baking dishes, greased

Plastic wrap

Aluminum foil

1. Brown beef, bell peppers, onions, and garlic in a large stockpot over medium heat until beef is no longer pink, about 30 minutes. Drain and discard fat. Stir in picante sauce, tomato sauce, beans, cumin, and salt.

2. Spread 4 cups of the meat mixture over the bottom of each baking dish. Cover the mixture with 6 corn tortillas, overlapping the edges as necessary to fit in a single layer. Spread 1 cup of cheese over the tortillas. Repeat each layer, finishing with a cheese topping.

3. Wrap each dish entirely in plastic wrap. Top with foil, label, and freeze.

FOIL PANS

In our recipes that call for freezing the food in baking dishes, reusable or disposable foil pans work well, and they're a perfect choice if you'll be sharing or giving away the food.

TO COOK ONE ENTRÉE

1. Completely thaw one dish in the refrigerator.

2. Preheat the oven to 350°F.

3. Remove plastic wrap and foil from baking dish and replace foil. Bake for 40 minutes, or until center is hot and edges are bubbly.

MEXICAN CHEESE BLENDS

Mexican-style cheese blends are available in the supermarket refrigerator case among the shredded cheese products. You can use a simple blend of Cheddar and Monterey Jack, or, for extra spice, choose a more exotic blend of several types of cheese labeled Mexican Blend or Mexican Style.

For years I was told by others that I could bake lasagna without boiling the noodles first. I refused to believe it. Not just set in my ways, I wasn't willing to take the chance of wasting the food if the noodles turned out chewy — or worse. One day after boiling 108 lasagna noodles for 12 lasagnas, I decided there had to be a better way. To my delight, not boiling the noodles worked out great! Using plenty of red sauce and freezing the entrée first creates the perfect noodles. Lasagna has never been so easy! —LT

CLASSIC LASAGNA: LARGE PAN

MAKES 2 ENTRÉES, 12 SERVINGS EACH

1 (48-ounce) container cottage cheese (about 6 cups)

4 eggs, lightly beaten

3 cups shredded Parmesan cheese, divided into 2 cups and 1 cup

13 cups Basic Red Sauce (page 178)

18 lasagna noodles, uncooked

2 pounds lean ground beef, cooked and drained

8 cups shredded mozzarella cheese (about 2 pounds)

Two 13- by 9- by 2-inch baking dishes (or deeper)

Plastic wrap

Aluminum foil

1. Combine cottage cheese, eggs, and 2 cups of the Parmesan in a large bowl.

2. Lay baking dishes before you and spread ½ cup red sauce in the bottom of each.

3. Assemble both lasagnas at once in layers in the following order:

LAYER 1

3 uncooked noodles

2 cups red sauce

1 cup cooked ground beef

1½ cups cottage cheese mixture

1 cup mozzarella

LAYER 2

3 uncooked noodles

2 cups red sauce

1 cup cooked ground beef — or whatever remains

1½ cups cottage cheese mixture — or whatever remains

1 cup mozzarella

LAYER 3

3 uncooked noodles

2 cups red sauce — or whatever remains

2 cups mozzarella

½ cup Parmesan

4. Wrap each dish entirely in plastic wrap. Top with foil, label, and freeze.

TO COOK ONE ENTRÉE

1. Thaw one entrée in the refrigerator or bake it straight from the freezer.

2. Preheat the oven to 375°F.

3. Remove plastic wrap and foil from baking dish and replace foil. Place dish on a rimmed baking sheet and bake for 1 hour if thawed, 1½ hours if frozen. Remove foil and continue baking until lasagna is bubbling and cheese is browned.

LASAGNA NOODLES

Although "no boil" or "oven ready" noodles are readily available, they aren't necessary in our lasagna recipes. The regular lasagna noodles are much less expensive and cook up perfectly when assembled uncooked in the lasagna.

You will notice that the lasagna recipes do not use an entire tray of ground beef. You could certainly triple the recipes to use the entire tray, or use the rest of the ground beef for another recipe. These smaller lasagnas are the perfect size for giving away. —LT

CLASSIC LASAGNA: SMALL PAN

MAKES 4 ENTRÉES, 4–6 SERVINGS EACH

1 (48-ounce) container cottage cheese (about 6 cups)

4 eggs, lightly beaten

3 cups shredded Parmesan cheese, divided into 2 cups and 1 cup

13 cups Basic Red Sauce (page 178)

24 lasagna noodles, uncooked

2 pounds lean ground beef, cooked and drained

8 cups shredded mozzarella cheese (about 2 pounds)

Four 12½- by 6½- by 3-inch foil loaf pans

Plastic wrap

Aluminum foil

1. Combine cottage cheese, eggs, and 2 cups of the Parmesan in a large bowl.

2. Lay baking dishes before you and spread ¼ cup red sauce in the bottom of each.

3. Assemble all four lasagnas at once in layers in the following order:

LAYER 1
2 uncooked noodles
1 cup red sauce
½ cup cooked ground beef
¾ cup cottage cheese mixture
½ cup mozzarella

LAYER 2
2 uncooked noodles
1 cup red sauce
½ cup cooked ground beef – or whatever remains

¾ cup cottage cheese mixture – or whatever remains
½ cup mozzarella

LAYER 3
2 uncooked noodles
1 cup red sauce – or whatever remains
1 cup mozzarella
¼ cup Parmesan

4. Wrap each dish entirely in plastic wrap. Top with foil, label, and freeze.

TO COOK ONE ENTRÉE

1. Thaw one entrée in the refrigerator or bake it straight from the freezer.

2. Preheat the oven to 375°F.

3. Remove plastic wrap and foil from baking dish and replace foil. Bake for 45 minutes if thawed, 1 hour if frozen. Remove foil and continue baking until lasagna is bubbling and cheese is browned.

WAREHOUSE BARGAINS

The recipe for the red sauce used in this and other recipes throughout the book takes advantage of the economy of warehouse packaging. We use the large cans (often called #10 cans) of tomato sauce, diced tomatoes and tomato paste that can be found at the warehouse clubs for substantially less money than the equivalent in smaller cans from the grocery store. Would you believe that you can buy a 106-ounce can of tomato sauce at the warehouse for less than the cost of a 29-ounce can at the grocery store? The savings are amazing! And it's always good to have some extra red sauce in the freezer.

Why not spice up those burgers with some gourmet seasoned sausages? Not only are these burgers tasty, but they're also a cinch to prepare — wonderful fare for a lazy summer evening. —KN

HABANERO AND CHILI HAMBURGERS

MAKES 4 ENTRÉES, 6 SERVINGS EACH

1 TRAY (ABOUT 6 POUNDS) LEAN GROUND BEEF

12 habanero and green chili–flavored sausages, or other spicy sausages

Plastic wrap

Wax paper

4 one-gallon freezer bags, labeled

1. Remove and discard casings from sausage and crumble meat into a large bowl. Add beef and, using your hands, mix until well combined.

2. Divide meat into 24 equal portions; form into patties. Place patties in a single layer on a rimmed baking sheet. Cover baking sheet with plastic wrap and freeze for 1 hour.

3. Divide frozen patties evenly among freezer bags, separating layers with wax paper. Discard plastic wrap. Seal and refreeze.

TO COOK ONE ENTRÉE

Prepare on an outdoor grill or indoors under a broiler.

1. Remove desired number of patties from the freezer. Place on a plate and thaw completely in the refrigerator.

FOR OUTDOOR COOKING

1. Prepare a medium-low fire on a gas or charcoal grill.

2. Cook burgers 5 to 6 minutes per side, or until an instant-read thermometer inserted into the thickest part of a patty reads 160°F.

FOR INDOOR COOKING

1. Arrange burgers on a broiler pan.

2. Broil patties under high heat for 5 minutes on each side, or until internal temperature reaches 160°F.

I have an aunt who is so capable and efficient, she makes everything she does look easy. Once, when I was at her home with my daughters having them fitted for the bridesmaid dresses she was making, our visit extended into the dinner hour. She insisted we stay, though she hadn't planned on having four more mouths to feed. She had exactly what was needed for this recipe. I usually need the benefit of planning, so I adapted her recipe for my own method. This has become one of my favorites. —LT

SPANISH RICE

MAKES 6 ENTRÉES, 6—8 SERVINGS EACH

1 TRAY (ABOUT 6 POUNDS) LEAN GROUND BEEF

24 cups Basic Red Sauce (page 178)

12 cups cooked white or brown rice, cooled (about 4 cups, uncooked)

1 large onion, chopped

2 green bell peppers, chopped

3 (2¼-ounce) cans sliced black olives (about 1½ cups)

12 cups shredded Cheddar cheese (about 3 pounds)

12 one-gallon freezer bags, label 6

6 one-quart freezer bags

1. Brown beef in a large stockpot over medium heat until no longer pink, about 20 minutes. Drain and discard fat. Cool beef. Divide evenly among the unlabeled 1-gallon freezer bags.

2. Into each bag of meat, measure 4 cups red sauce and 2 cups cooked rice. Divide the onion, bell peppers, and olives evenly among the bags of meat and rice.

3. Seal bags and massage gently to distribute the ingredients.

4. Divide the cheese evenly among the 1-quart freezer bags and seal. Place one bag of meat and rice mixture and one bag of cheese into each labeled 1-gallon bag.

5. Seal and freeze.

TO COOK ONE ENTRÉE

1. Completely thaw one entrée in the refrigerator.

2. Preheat the oven to 350°F.

3. Put meat and rice mixture in an ungreased baking dish and sprinkle with the cheese. Bake, covered, for 30 to 40 minutes, or until sauce is bubbling and cheese is melted.

This dish takes a little extra time to prepare, but with its festive flavors and colors, it's worth it. Serve with sour cream, guacamole, or blue corn chips to highlight the peppers' intense red color. —KN

MEXI-STUFFED PEPPERS

MAKES 4 ENTRÉES, 6 SERVINGS EACH

1 TRAY (ABOUT 6 POUNDS) LEAN GROUND BEEF

2 cups diced onion
(about 2 medium)

¼ cup minced garlic
(about 36 cloves)

4 cups frozen corn

4 cups cooked rice, cooled
(about 1⅓ cups uncooked)

4 (15-ounce) cans tomato sauce
(8 cups)

1 cup taco seasoning, such as Penzey's Bold Taco Seasoning

4 one-gallon freezer bags, labeled

ON HAND FOR COOKING EACH ENTRÉE

6 red bell peppers

1 cup shredded Mexican cheese blend

1. Brown beef, onion, and garlic in a large stockpot over medium heat until beef is no longer pink, about 30 minutes. Drain and discard fat. Cool beef. Stir in corn, rice, tomato sauce, and taco seasoning. Divide mixture evenly among the freezer bags.

2. Seal and freeze.

TO COOK ONE ENTRÉE

1. Completely thaw one entrée in the refrigerator.

2. Preheat the oven to 350°F.

3. Prepare peppers for stuffing: wash, cut off tops, and seed peppers. Fill each with meat mixture. Sprinkle with cheese. Place on a greased rimmed baking sheet. Bake for 35 minutes, or until filling is hot.

MAKE IT VEGETARIAN

Make a meatless variation of this dish by using a soybean substitute (such as Morningstar Farms Crumbles or Boca Meatless Ground Burger) in place of the beef. Instead of adding at the beginning, however, the beef substitute is added to the mixture just before stuffing the peppers. Make the sauce and freeze it as directed, omitting the ground beef. After the sauce has thawed, mix in 3 cups ground beef substitute. Fill each pepper and bake as directed.

These delicious morsels drenched in a barbecue-style sauce have a surprise pocket of cheese inside. Some of the participants in my cooking sessions claim that they have had to referee at the dinner table to decide who gets the last meatball! —LT

MOZZARELLA MEATBALLS

MAKES 6 ENTRÉES, ABOUT 20 MEATBALLS EACH

MEATBALLS

1 TRAY (ABOUT 6 POUNDS) LEAN GROUND BEEF

15 mozzarella string cheese, or a 1-pound block of mozzarella cut into 120 cubes

3 cups dry bread crumbs

⅔ cup milk

4 eggs, lightly beaten

¼ cup minced onion

2 tablespoons minced garlic (about 18 cloves)

1 tablespoon salt

2 teaspoons black pepper

SAUCE

4 cups ketchup

2 cups red wine vinegar

2 cups Worcestershire sauce

2 cups packed brown sugar

2 tablespoons minced garlic (about 18 cloves)

2 tablespoons minced onion

1 tablespoon dry mustard

2 teaspoons black pepper

6 one-gallon freezer bags, labeled

1. Remove string cheese from wrappers and cut each string into 8 equal pieces. Place in a large bowl or 1-gallon freezer bag and freeze until it is time to form meatballs.

2. Preheat the oven to 500°F.

3. Using your hands, thoroughly combine beef, breadcrumbs, milk, eggs, onion, garlic, salt, and pepper in a large bowl. Shape into 1- to 1½- inch meatballs, around each piece of frozen mozzarella. Seal meatballs well to keep cheese from oozing out.

4. Place meatballs close together on lightly greased broiler pans or rimmed baking sheets. Bake for 15 minutes. Cool meatballs.

5. While meatballs are baking and cooling, mix ketchup, vinegar, Worcestershire sauce, brown sugar, garlic, onion, mustard, and pepper in a large bowl. Divide sauce evenly among the freezer bags. Divide cooled meatballs evenly among bags of sauce.

6. Seal and freeze.

TO COOK ONE ENTRÉE

1. Completely thaw one entrée in the refrigerator.

2. Preheat the oven to 350°F.

3. Pour meatballs and sauce into an ungreased baking dish. Bake, uncovered, for 30 minutes, or until meatballs are heated through. Serve over rice or noodles.

WAREHOUSE BARGAINS

Ketchup can be had for two and a half times cheaper per ounce when purchased in the large cans at the warehouse versus the bottles at the grocery store. Use what you need in this and other recipes and store the rest in a clean container with an air-tight lid in the refrigerator. You can even wash and re-use your glass grocery store ketchup bottles.

Although a big fan of cooking from scratch, my mouth still waters when I think about meaty pork chops braised in a skillet with a can of cream of mushroom soup added to make a tasty gravy. I feel a little sheepish admitting that it's a dish I've always liked. This is my answer to the craving for that dish. It has much better flavor, and when made ahead and frozen, it's just as quick to make for dinner as opening a can of soup. Making the sauce from scratch gives you ultimate control in ingredient selection. —LT

SALISBURY MEATBALLS

MAKES 6 ENTRÉES, ABOUT 20 MEATBALLS EACH

MEATBALLS

1 TRAY (ABOUT 6 POUNDS) LEAN GROUND BEEF

3 cups dry bread crumbs

⅔ cup milk

4 eggs, lightly beaten

¼ cup minced onion

2 tablespoons minced garlic (about 18 cloves)

1 tablespoon salt

2 teaspoons black pepper

SAUCE

1 cup (2 sticks) butter

1½ pounds fresh white mushrooms, cleaned and sliced

1 cup all-purpose flour

8 cups water

4 cups half-and-half (or light cream)

2 tablespoons Worcestershire sauce

2 tablespoons beef bouillon granules

1½ teaspoons black pepper

6 one-gallon freezer bags, labeled

1. Preheat the oven to 500°F.

2. Using your hands, thoroughly combine beef, bread-crumbs, milk, eggs, onion, garlic, salt, and pepper in a large bowl. Shape into 1- to 1½-inch meatballs, placing them close together on lightly greased broiler pans or rimmed baking sheets. Bake for 15 minutes, or until an instant-read thermometer inserted into the center of a meatball reads 160°F. Cool meatballs.

3. While the meatballs are baking and cooling, melt butter in a large stockpot over medium heat. Add mushrooms and cook, stirring, until soft, about 7 minutes. Stir in flour. Mixture will be lumpy. Cook, stirring, for 2 minutes. Gradually stir in water and half-and-half; cook, stirring, until sauce thickens, about 15 minutes. Whisk to make a smooth sauce. Add Worcestershire sauce, bouillon, and pepper; stir. Cool sauce.

4. Divide cooled meatballs and sauce evenly among the freezer bags.

5. Seal and freeze.

TO COOK ONE ENTRÉE

Completely thaw one entrée in the refrigerator. Prepare on the stove or in the oven.

STOVE TOP

Bring meatballs and sauce to a simmer in a large skillet over medium heat until meatballs are heated through. Do not boil.

OVEN

Preheat the oven to 350°F. Pour meatballs and sauce into an ungreased baking dish and bake, uncovered, for 30 minutes, or until meatballs are heated through.

Serve over rice, mashed potatoes, or noodles.

THICK AND THIN

If the sauce seems thin before freezing it, resist the temptation to thicken it with more flour. When the entrée comes out of the freezer and is reheated, the sauce will be considerably thicker than it was before freezing.

These meatballs are perfect over rice or on their own as a potluck dish. For guests who like a bit of zip, I offer chopped scallions and a little hot chili paste when I serve this dish. —LT

SWEET-AND-SOUR MEATBALLS

MAKES 6 ENTRÉES, ABOUT 20 MEATBALLS EACH

MEATBALLS

1 TRAY (ABOUT 6 POUNDS) LEAN GROUND BEEF

3 cups dry bread crumbs

⅔ cup milk

4 eggs, lightly beaten

¼ cup minced onion

2 tablespoons minced garlic (about 18 cloves)

1 tablespoon salt

2 teaspoons black pepper

SAUCE

2 cups packed brown sugar

½ cup cornstarch

1 (106-ounce) can pineapple tidbits, drained, juice reserved

½ cup soy sauce

2½ cups red wine vinegar

6 one-gallon freezer bags, labeled

1. Preheat the oven to 500°F.

2. Using your hands, thoroughly combine beef, bread-crumbs, milk, eggs, onion, garlic, salt, and pepper in a large bowl. Shape into 1- to 1½-inch meatballs, placing finished pieces close together on lightly greased broiler pans or rimmed baking sheets. Bake for 15 minutes, or until an instant-read thermometer inserted into the center of a meatball reads 160°F. Cool meatballs.

3. While the meatballs are baking and cooling, mix the brown sugar and cornstarch in a large stockpot. Add pineapple juice, soy sauce, and vinegar; stir. Cook over medium heat, stirring occasionally, until sauce thickens, about 20 minutes. Cool sauce.

4. Divide cooled meatballs and sauce evenly among the freezer bags. Divide drained pineapple tidbits evenly among the bags of meatballs and sauce.

5. Seal and freeze.

TO COOK ONE ENTRÉE

Completely thaw one entrée in the refrigerator. Prepare in the oven or in a slow cooker.

OVEN

Preheat the oven to 350°F. Put meatballs and sauce in an ungreased baking dish and bake, uncovered, for 30 minutes, or until meatballs are heated through.

SLOW COOKER

Put meatballs and sauce in a slow cooker. Cook on low for 2 to 5 hours, or until meatballs are heated through.

A VARIETY OF VEGETABLES

If you wish, add bite-size pieces of raw green bell pepper, onion, or carrot to the bags along with the pineapple tidbits before sealing and freezing.

You may already have a chili recipe you like, but this one is always a huge hit. Offer toppings of shredded Cheddar cheese, sour cream, chopped scallions, and sliced black olives. Serve corn bread on the side. —LT

CLASSIC CHILI

MAKES 4 ENTRÉES, 8 SERVINGS EACH

1 TRAY (ABOUT 6 POUNDS) LEAN GROUND BEEF

4 cups chopped onion (about 4 medium)

1 tablespoon minced garlic (about 9 cloves)

12 cups Basic Red Sauce (page 178)

8 (15-ounce) cans kidney beans

4 (15-ounce) cans pork and beans

4 tablespoons chili powder

4 tablespoons hot pepper sauce

4 teaspoons dried oregano

4 teaspoons black pepper

4 one-gallon freezer bags, labeled

1. Brown beef, onion, and garlic in a large stockpot over medium heat until beef is no longer pink, about 30 minutes. Drain and discard fat. Cool beef; divide evenly among the freezer bags.

2. Into each bag measure 3 cups red sauce, 2 cans kidney beans, 1 can pork and beans, 1 tablespoon chili powder, 1 tablespoon hot pepper sauce, 1 teaspoon oregano, and 1 teaspoon pepper.

3. Seal and freeze.

TO COOK ONE ENTRÉE

1. Completely thaw one entrée in the refrigerator.

2. Cook, stirring occasionally, in a medium saucepan over low heat for 1 hour, or until liquid cooks off and chili is thick.

TURNING DOWN THE HEAT

If you're cooking for people who are sensitive to spicy foods, leave out the hot pepper sauce. The resulting chili is still delicious. For those who like it hot, pass the pepper sauce at the table.

This recipe is named for all the ingredients that start with the letter *B*. I greatly value the contribution of my local growers, producers, bakers, vintners, and brewers. If you live near a microbrewery, feel free to substitute their porter for the Oregon-brewed porter I use. If you don't have a local brewer, try a local mustard or make your own ketchup, or try a new balsamic vinegar — there's more than one way to incorporate local flavors into this recipe. Be adventurous. —KN

4 Bs FLANK STEAK

MAKES 2 ENTRÉES, 6 SERVINGS EACH

1 TRAY (ABOUT 3 POUNDS, TWO STEAKS) FLANK STEAKS

1½ cups Black Butte Porter, or other dark beer

½ cup ketchup

¼ cup packed dark brown sugar

¼ cup balsamic vinegar

¼ cup Dijon mustard

2 teaspoons minced garlic (about 6 cloves)

½ teaspoon black pepper

2 one-gallon freezer bags, labeled

1. Rinse and trim steaks as desired. Put one steak in each freezer bag.

2. Whisk together beer, ketchup, brown sugar, vinegar, and mustard in a medium bowl. Divide marinade evenly over the steaks. Into each bag measure 1 teaspoon garlic and ¼ teaspoon pepper.

3. Seal and freeze.

TO COOK ONE ENTRÉE

1. Completely thaw one entrée in the refrigerator.

2. Prepare a medium fire in a gas or charcoal grill.

3. Cook steak for 15 to 20 minutes for medium-rare to medium. Turn occasionally and baste as desired. Do not baste during final 5 minutes of cooking. Discard remaining marinade.

This is a contribution from our colleague Shawnee. Molasses, her inspiration for this recipe, imparts a distinct flavor that remains after cooking. If you reduce the molasses, the sweet-spicy flavor of the nutmeg will become more apparent. Adjust the flavors to your liking. —KN / LT

BLACKJACK STEAK

MAKES 2 ENTRÉES, 6 SERVINGS EACH

1 TRAY (ABOUT 3 POUNDS, TWO STEAKS) FLANK STEAKS

1 cup balsamic vinegar

1 cup molasses

3 teaspoons dried thyme

1 teaspoon salt

½ teaspoon black pepper

½ teaspoon ground nutmeg

4 teaspoons minced garlic (about 12 cloves)

2 one-gallon freezer bags, labeled

1. Rinse and trim steaks as desired. Put one steak in each freezer bag.

2. Whisk together vinegar, molasses, thyme, salt, pepper, and nutmeg in a medium bowl. Divide the marinade evenly over the steaks. Into each bag measure 2 teaspoons minced garlic.

3. Seal and freeze.

TO COOK ONE ENTRÉE

1. Completely thaw one entrée in the refrigerator.

2. Prepare a medium fire in a gas or charcoal grill.

3. Cook steak for 15 to 20 minutes for medium-rare to medium. Turn occasionally and baste as desired. Do not baste during final 5 minutes of cooking. Discard remaining marinade.

SAFE COOKING TEMPERATURES

Cases of food-borne illness seem to be in the news regularly. One of the best ways to prevent illness is to make sure your meats are thoroughly cooked, meeting temperature levels recommended by food safety experts. For steaks, the internal temperature should reach 145°F. By that time, the outside of the steak will have reached 160°F, the temperature necessary to avoid food-borne illness.

Portland, Oregon, is called the "Rose City." It and many other cities on the Pacific rim in North America enjoy the culinary influence of our Asian neighbors. Often the flavors are "Americanized" or blended with other ethnic cuisines. The orange juice and rosemary in this teriyaki dish set it apart. —KN

ROSE CITY TERIYAKI

MAKES 2 ENTRÉES, 6 SERVINGS EACH

1 TRAY (ABOUT 3 POUNDS, TWO STEAKS) FLANK STEAKS

½ cup teriyaki sauce

½ cup toasted sesame oil

¼ cup orange juice

2 tablespoons soy sauce

2 teaspoons salt

1 cup chopped onion (about 1 medium)

1 tablespoon dried rosemary

2 teaspoons minced garlic

½ teaspoon crushed red pepper flakes

2 one-gallon freezer bags, labeled

1. Rinse and trim steaks as desired. Put one steak in each freezer bag.

2. Whisk together teriyaki sauce, sesame oil, orange juice, soy sauce, and salt in a medium bowl. Divide the marinade evenly over the steaks. Into each bag measure ½ cup onion, ½ tablespoon rosemary, 1 teaspoon garlic, and ¼ teaspoon crushed red pepper.

3. Seal and freeze.

TO COOK ONE ENTRÉE

1. Completely thaw one entrée in the refrigerator.

2. Prepare a medium fire in a gas or charcoal grill.

3. Cook steak for 15 to 20 minutes for medium-rare to medium. Turn occasionally and baste as desired. Do not baste during final 5 minutes of cooking. Discard remaining marinade.

You'll know how good these fajitas are going to taste when you smell the marinade. It's out of this world! If you want to stretch this meal farther, add refried beans to the stir-fried beef and vegetables and roll into burritos. —LT

BEEF FAJITAS

MAKES 4 ENTRÉES, 4 SERVINGS EACH

1 TRAY (ABOUT 6 POUNDS) BONELESS TOP SIRLOIN STEAKS

½ cup lime juice

½ cup soy sauce

½ cup vegetable oil

2 teaspoons ground cumin

2 teaspoons dried oregano

2 teaspoons chili powder

1 teaspoon black pepper

8 teaspoons minced garlic (about 24 cloves)

4 large onions, cut into strips

4 large green bell peppers, cut into strips

4 cups shredded Cheddar cheese (about 1 pound)

40 flour tortillas

4 two-gallon freezer bags, labeled

8 one-gallon freezer bags

8 one-quart freezer bags

ON HAND FOR COOKING EACH ENTRÉE

2 teaspoons vegetable oil

Sour cream, salsa, guacamole, or other fajita toppings

1. Rinse steaks and trim excess fat. Cutting across the grain, slice each steak into narrow strips. Divide beef evenly among four 1-gallon bags.

2. Whisk together lime juice, soy sauce, oil, cumin, oregano, chili powder, and black pepper in a medium bowl. Divide the marinade evenly over the beef. Into each bag of beef strips measure 2 teaspoons garlic. Seal.

3. Divide onion and green pepper strips evenly among four 1-quart bags. Seal. Measure 1 cup cheese into each of the remaining 1-quart bags. Seal. Put 10 tortillas into each of the remaining 1-gallon bags. Seal.

4. Into each of the 2-gallon bags, place a bag of beef in marinade, a bag of onions and peppers, a bag of cheese, and a bag of tortillas.

5. Seal and freeze.

TO COOK ONE ENTRÉE

1. Completely thaw one entrée in the refrigerator.

2. Heat oil in a large skillet over medium-high heat. Add onions and peppers and stir-fry until soft, about 3 minutes. Remove vegetables from skillet and add beef. Stir-fry beef until well browned, about 10 minutes. Remove pan from heat and return vegetables, stirring to combine. Serve with tortillas and cheese. Add fajita toppings as desired.

JUMBO BAGS FOR BIG STORAGE JOBS

Two-gallon freezer bags can be tricky to find, but they're worth having for this recipe. I use the Albertsons store brand. They're the best quality at the best price that I've found. If you can't find 2-gallon freezer bags, 2-gallon storage bags are an acceptable substitute. If you have no 2-gallon bags at all, wrap each complete entrée in a plastic grocery bag and clearly label. The outer bag can be re-used.

My children are not big meat eaters, so you can imagine my surprise when my two preschoolers ate a third of a steak by themselves. Of all my recipes, this is their favorite. —KN

SESAME-SOY SIRLOIN

MAKES 3 ENTRÉES, 4 SERVINGS EACH

1 TRAY (ABOUT 6 POUNDS) BONELESS TOP SIRLOIN STEAKS

½ cup soy sauce

¼ cup lime juice

2 tablespoons toasted sesame oil

2 tablespoons brown sugar

3 tablespoons minced ginger

3 tablespoons minced garlic (about 27 cloves)

3 tablespoons sesame seeds

3 teaspoons crushed red pepper flakes

¾ teaspoon black pepper

3 one-gallon freezer bags, labeled

1. Rinse and divide steaks evenly among the freezer bags.

2. Whisk together soy sauce, lime juice, sesame oil, and brown sugar in a medium bowl until the sugar dissolves. Divide the marinade evenly over the steaks. Into each bag measure 1 tablespoon ginger, 1 tablespoon garlic, 1 tablespoon sesame seeds, 1 teaspoon crushed red pepper, and ¼ teaspoon black pepper.

3. Seal and freeze.

TO COOK ONE ENTRÉE

1. Completely thaw one entrée in the refrigerator.

2. Prepare a medium fire in a gas or charcoal grill.

3. Cook steak for 14 to 18 minutes for medium-rare to medium. Turn occasionally and baste as desired. Do not baste during final 5 minutes of cooking. Discard remaining marinade.

The flavor of sesame, the tang of cranberry, and the sweet surprise of mandarin orange make this stir-fry special. It is delicious served over your favorite rice. —KN / LT

SHANGHAI STIR-FRY

MAKES 3 ENTRÉES, 6 SERVINGS EACH

1 TRAY (ABOUT 6 POUNDS) BONELESS TOP SIRLOIN STEAKS

⅔ cup cranberry juice

½ cup soy sauce

½ cup packed brown sugar

3 teaspoons minced garlic (about 9 cloves)

3 teaspoons minced ginger

1½ teaspoons crushed red pepper flakes

Zest of one orange

3 one-gallon freezer bags, labeled

ON HAND FOR COOKING EACH ENTRÉE

2 teaspoons vegetable oil

1 (11-ounce) can mandarin orange slices, drained

2 teaspoons sesame seeds

1. Rinse steaks and trim excess fat. Cutting across the grain, slice each steak into narrow strips. Divide beef evenly among the freezer bags.

2. Whisk together cranberry juice, soy sauce, and brown sugar in a medium bowl. Divide the marinade evenly over the beef. Into each bag, measure 1 teaspoon garlic, 1 teaspoon ginger, and ½ teaspoon crushed red pepper. Divide the orange zest evenly among the three bags.

3. Seal and freeze.

TO COOK ONE ENTRÉE

1. Completely thaw one entrée in the refrigerator.

2. Pour off the marinade and reserve. Heat oil in a large skillet over medium-high heat. Add beef and stir-fry until well browned, about 10 minutes. Remove beef from pan and keep warm. Add marinade to skillet, reduce heat, and simmer for 3 minutes. Return beef to pan. Add mandarin oranges and stir to coat. Sprinkle with sesame seeds.

This is a Tkacsik family favorite! If you love blue cheese and want to skip the steak, the sauce is also tasty over pasta. —LT

STEAK SKEWERS
WITH BLUE CHEESE DIPPING SAUCE

MAKES 3 ENTRÉES, 4 SERVINGS EACH

1 TRAY (ABOUT 6 POUNDS) BONELESS TOP SIRLOIN STEAKS

½ cup olive oil

¼ cup red wine vinegar

1½ teaspoons black pepper

SAUCE

1 (4- to 5-ounce) container crumbled blue cheese (about ¾ cup)

3 cups heavy cream

¾ teaspoon black pepper

6 one-gallon freezer bags, label 3

3 one-quart freezer bags

ON HAND FOR COOKING EACH ENTRÉE

8 (9-inch) wooden or metal skewers

1. Rinse steaks and trim excess fat. Cut into 1-inch cubes. Divide beef evenly among the unlabeled 1-gallon freezer bags.

2. Whisk together oil and vinegar in a small bowl. Divide the marinade evenly over the beef. Into each bag, measure ½ teaspoon pepper. Seal bags.

3. Divide the blue cheese among the three 1-quart freezer bags. Into each bag of cheese, measure 1 cup heavy cream and ¼ teaspoon pepper. Seal bags.

4. Into each labeled 1-gallon bag, place one bag of beef and one bag of sauce.

5. Seal and freeze.

TO COOK ONE ENTRÉE

Prepare on an outdoor grill or indoors under a broiler.

1. Completely thaw one entrée in the refrigerator.

FOR OUTDOOR COOKING

1. Prepare a medium fire in a gas or charcoal grill.

2. If using wooden skewers, soak them in water while beef is thawing. Thread steak pieces onto skewers. Grill, turning occasionally, about 10 minutes or until beef is done to your liking. Discard remaining marinade.

3. Meanwhile, heat the blue cheese mixture in a medium saucepan over medium heat. Simmer gently, stirring frequently, until the cream reduces and thickens into a velvety sauce. Serve as a dipping sauce with the steak skewers.

FOR INDOOR COOKING

1. Arrange skewers, prepared as above, on an ungreased broiler pan. Broil steak under high heat, 5 inches from the heat source, turning frequently for about 10 minutes or until beef is done to your liking. Discard remaining marinade.

2. Heat and serve the cheese sauce as described above.

I think the secret to this delicious soup is our Basic Red Sauce. The large pot of soup this recipe yields is perfect when company comes. I like to put the frozen soup in the slow cooker on a Sunday morning and turn it on high. By the time we get home from church, it's ready to eat. I can invite last-minute lunch guests with no worry about what to serve. Now, if only I could be sure the house would be clean! —LT

BEEF BARLEY SOUP

MAKES 4 ENTRÉES, 6–8 SERVINGS EACH

1 PACKAGE (ABOUT 6 POUNDS) SIRLOIN TIP BEEF OR OTHER BEEF SUITABLE FOR SLOW COOKING

6 cups sliced carrots (about 12 medium)

6 cups sliced celery (about 12 stalks)

4 cups chopped onion (about 4 medium)

2 large green bell peppers, cut into 1-inch pieces

4 (14½-ounce) cans diced tomatoes with juice (about 8 cups)

4 cups Basic Red Sauce (page 178)

4 tablespoons beef bouillon granules

4 teaspoons salt

2 teaspoons black pepper

2 cups (1 one-pound bag) pearl barley

8 one-gallon freezer bags, label 4

4 one-quart freezer bags

1. Rinse and trim beef as desired. Cut into bite-size pieces. Divide beef evenly among the unlabeled 1-gallon bags.

2. Into each of the four bags of beef measure 1½ cups carrots, 1½ cups celery, 1 cup onion, one-fourth of the bell peppers, 1 can tomatoes with juice, 1 cup red sauce, 1 tablespoon bouillon, 1 teaspoon salt, ½ teaspoon black pepper. Seal.

3. Into each of the 1-quart bags measure ½ cup barley. Seal. Place one bag of soup and one bag of barley into each of the four labeled 1-gallon bags.

4. Seal and freeze.

TO COOK ONE ENTRÉE

Put frozen soup into slow cooker. (Soup doesn't need to be thawed.) Add 4 cups of water and the bag of barley. Cook on low for 8 to 10 hours or on high for 4 to 5 hours, or until the meat and vegetables are tender.

This beef dish has a subtle flavor, suitable for everyone. —LT

GINGER BEEF

MAKES 3 ENTRÉES, 6 SERVINGS EACH

1 PACKAGE (ABOUT 6 POUNDS) SIRLOIN TIP BEEF OR OTHER BEEF SUITABLE FOR SLOW COOKING

3 cups water

9 scallions, chopped (about 1½ cups)

¾ cup soy sauce

6 teaspoons beef bouillon granules

6 teaspoons minced ginger

6 teaspoons minced garlic

3 one-gallon freezer bags

1. Rinse and trim beef as desired. Cut into thick strips, about 2 by 5 inches. (The beef should not be in bite-size pieces.) Divide beef evenly among the 1-gallon freezer bags.

2. Into each bag of beef measure 1 cup water, ½ cup scallions, ¼ cup soy sauce, 2 teaspoons bouillon, 2 teaspoons ginger, and 2 teaspoons garlic.

3. Seal and freeze.

TO COOK ONE ENTRÉE

1. Thaw one entrée in the refrigerator or cook it straight from the freezer.

2. Put beef and broth into slow cooker. Cook on low for 5 to 6 hours, or until beef is fork tender.

BUYING TIPS

Packages of this cut of beef can vary in size by several pounds. Buy as close to 6 pounds as possible, or, alternatively, in multiples of 3 pounds, and adjust the recipe accordingly. Because you're measuring ingredients into each bag separately, you can easily alter the number of entrées you make.

When my husband was in graduate school, we rarely ate out. On a tight budget, I began to develop recipes in imitation of our favorite restaurant meals. It became a challenge to create and test dishes, matching wits with the chefs. This particular recipe is so superior to any we ever ordered, it became the one we craved instead of the restaurant version. —LT

CHEESE STEAKS

MAKES 3 ENTRÉES, 6 SERVINGS EACH

1 PACKAGE (ABOUT 6 POUNDS) SIRLOIN TIP BEEF OR OTHER BEEF SUITABLE FOR SLOW COOKING

6 teaspoons beef bouillon granules

3 cups water

3 large green bell peppers, cut into strips

3 large onions, cut into strips

18 slices deli cheese (Cheddar, Monterey Jack, or Swiss)

18 long bread rolls

3 *two-gallon freezer bags, labeled*

3 *one-gallon freezer bags*

3 *one-quart freezer bags*

Plastic wrap

ON HAND FOR COOKING EACH ENTRÉE

2 teaspoons vegetable oil

Foil

1. Rinse and trim beef as desired. Cut beef into three equal pieces. Place a piece of beef into each 1-gallon freezer bag. Into each bag measure 2 teaspoons bouillon and 1 cup water. Seal bags.

2. Divide bell peppers and onions evenly among the 1-quart freezer bags. Seal.

3. Divide cheese into three portions of 6 slices each; enclose in plastic wrap. Divide rolls into three portions of 6 each; enclose in plastic wrap.

4. Place a bag of beef, a bag of peppers and onions, a stack of cheese slices, and a packet of rolls inside each 2-gallon freezer bag.

5. Seal and freeze.

TO COOK ONE ENTRÉE

1. Thaw one entrée in the refrigerator or cook it straight from the freezer.

2. Put beef and broth into slow cooker. Cook on low for 5 to 6 hours, or until the beef is tender and pulls apart easily with a fork. Remove beef from broth and set aside until cool enough to shred. Reserve broth.

3. Preheat the oven to 350°F.

4. Meanwhile, heat oil in a large skillet over medium-high heat. Add peppers and onions and stir-fry until soft, about 3 minutes. Remove pan from heat. Slice and open rolls. Divide beef and vegetables evenly among the rolls. Place a slice of cheese inside each sandwich; close and wrap in foil. Heat in the oven for 10 minutes. Unwrap carefully. Serve with broth for dipping.

OPTIONAL FLAVOR BOOSTER

Try spreading some horseradish mayonnaise on the rolls before adding the beef.

CHAPTER THREE

PORK MAIN DISHES

On our vacation to the Oregon coast one summer, we happened upon a beer sale at a local microbrewery. My husband and I are home brewers and bargain hunters, so this was right up our alley! We found some new favorites. I modified the 4 Bs Flank Steak recipe (page 95) to use up one of the lighter ales we liked least. The dish turned out to be quite good. —KN

4 Bs GRILLED CHOPS

MAKES 2 ENTRÉES, 6 SERVINGS EACH

1 TRAY (6–8 POUNDS, OR 12 CHOPS) PORK LOIN CHOPS, BONELESS OR BONE-IN

1½ cups pale ale (or other light beer)

½ cup ketchup

¼ cup packed brown sugar

¼ cup white balsamic vinegar

¼ cup Dijon mustard

2 teaspoons minced garlic (about 6 cloves)

½ teaspoon black pepper

2 one-gallon freezer bags, labeled

1. Rinse and trim chops as desired. Divide the chops evenly between the two freezer bags.

2. Whisk together beer, ketchup, brown sugar, vinegar, and mustard In a medium bowl. Divide marinade evenly over the chops.

3. Into each bag, measure 1 teaspoon garlic and ¼ teaspoon pepper.

4. Seal and freeze.

NOTE: The chops and marinade can also be divided among three or more 1-gallon freezer bags to make more entrées with fewer portions.

TO COOK ONE ENTRÉE

1. Completely thaw one entrée in the refrigerator.

2. Prepare a medium-low fire in a gas or charcoal grill.

3. Cook chops until an instant-read thermometer inserted into the thickest part of a chop reads 160°F. Discard remaining marinade.

BALSAMIC VINEGAR

We have found that balsamic vinegar is one of the rare ingredients that offer no substantial savings when purchased at the warehouse versus the grocery store. Since prices are comparable between the two, choose your favorite brand at either location. If you use a lot of balsamic vinegar, you may want to purchase the warehouse bottles simply for the convenience of the size.

I named this recipe after a local bento shop owner I used to know. She and her son always served the most wonderful food with such great hospitality. I still recall An's wide, warm smile, greeting us each time we ate there. She came to know my family, my parents, and me, too. This dish is sure to put a smile on your dinner guests' faces, like it does mine — wonderful smiles that always remind me of An. —KN

AN'S PORK CHOPS

MAKES 3 ENTRÉES, 4 SERVINGS EACH

1 TRAY (6–8 POUNDS, OR 12 CHOPS) PORK LOIN CHOPS, BONELESS OR BONE-IN

1⅓ cups soy sauce

½ cup sugar

⅔ cup rice vinegar

¼ cup toasted sesame oil

3 tablespoons minced ginger

3 tablespoons minced garlic (about 27 cloves)

¾ teaspoon cayenne pepper

3 one-gallon freezer bags, labeled

1. Rinse and divide chops evenly among the freezer bags.

2. Combine soy sauce, sugar, vinegar, and sesame oil in a medium bowl. Divide marinade evenly over the pork.

3. Into each bag measure 1 tablespoon ginger, 1 tablespoon garlic, and ¼ teaspoon cayenne.

4. Seal and freeze.

TO COOK ONE ENTRÉE

1. Completely thaw one entrée in the refrigerator.

2. Prepare a medium-low fire in a gas or charcoal grill.

3. Cook chops until an instant-read thermometer inserted into the thickest part of a chop reads 160°F. Discard remaining marinade.

RICE VINEGAR

Rice vinegar can be found in the Asian food section of your grocery store. The strength of flavor among rice vinegars varies widely. If you find the flavors in this dish are unbalanced or have too heavy a vinegar taste, make a note to use less vinegar next time.

Look for this unique jelly at the farm stand or farmers' market, or in either the specialty aisle or near the peanut butter and preserves in a grocery store. Sweet with just a little kick, it adds a bit of fun to everyday pork chops. —KN / LT

PEPPER JELLY PORK CHOPS

MAKES 3 ENTRÉES, 4 SERVINGS EACH

1 TRAY (6–8 POUNDS, OR 12 CHOPS) PORK LOIN CHOPS, BONELESS OR BONE-IN

1 cup jalapeño pepper jelly, such as Tabasco brand

2 tablespoons spicy brown mustard

2 tablespoons balsamic vinegar

2 tablespoons olive oil

1½ teaspoons dried thyme

3 one-gallon freezer bags, labeled

1. Rinse and divide chops evenly among the freezer bags.

2. Whisk together pepper jelly, mustard, vinegar, oil, and thyme. Divide the marinade evenly over the chops.

3. Seal and freeze.

TO COOK ONE ENTRÉE

Prepare on an outdoor grill or indoors under a broiler.

1. Completely thaw one entrée in the refrigerator.

FOR OUTDOOR COOKING

1. Prepare a medium fire in a gas or charcoal grill.

2. Cook chops, turning occasionally, until an instant-read thermometer inserted into the thickest part of a chop reads 160°F. Baste the chops as desired. Do not baste during final 5 minutes of cooking. Discard remaining marinade.

FOR INDOOR COOKING

Arrange chops on a greased broiler pan. Broil chops under high heat 5 inches from the heat source, turning frequently, for 15 to 18 minutes, or until an instant-read thermometer inserted into the thickest part of a chop reads 160°F. Baste the chops as desired. Do not baste during final 5 minutes of cooking. Discard remaining marinade.

The marinade in this recipe is also our best-loved salad dressing. Make an extra batch to serve over salad greens — you may never buy commercial dressing again. —LT

BASIL-BALSAMIC CHOPS

MAKES 3 ENTRÉES, 4 SERVINGS EACH

1 TRAY (6–8 POUNDS, OR 12 CHOPS) PORK LOIN CHOPS, BONELESS OR BONE-IN

1 cup olive oil

½ cup balsamic vinegar

¼ cup soy sauce

¼ cup lemon juice

2 tablespoons honey

3 teaspoons minced garlic (about 9 cloves)

3 teaspoons dried basil

2¼ teaspoons black pepper

3 one-gallon freezer bags, labeled

1. Rinse and divide chops evenly among the freezer bags.

2. Whisk together olive oil, vinegar, soy sauce, lemon juice, and honey in a medium bowl. Divide marinade evenly over the pork.

3. Into each bag measure 1 teaspoon garlic, 1 teaspoon basil, and ¾ teaspoon pepper.

4. Seal and freeze.

TO COOK ONE ENTRÉE

Prepare on an outdoor grill or indoors under a broiler.

1. Completely thaw one entrée in the refrigerator.

FOR OUTDOOR COOKING

1. Prepare a medium fire in a gas or charcoal grill.

2. Cook chops, turning occasionally, until an instant-read thermometer inserted into the thickest part of a chop reads 160°F. Discard remaining marinade.

FOR INDOOR COOKING

Arrange chops on an ungreased broiler pan. Broil chops under high heat, 5 inches from the heat source, turning frequently, for 15 to 18 minutes or until an instant-read thermometer inserted into the thickest part of a chop reads 160°F. Discard remaining marinade.

A VERSATILE MARINADE

What else can you season with this delicious marinade? In addition to enjoying it as a salad dressing, you can substitute 1 tray pack (about 6 pounds) boneless, skinless chicken half-breasts for the pork chops and grill until an instant-read thermometer inserted in the thickest part of the chicken reads 170°F.

CREATIVE LEFTOVERS

Your leftovers will not always stretch into another full meal, but you can still find a delicious use for them. The flavors in most of our chicken, beef, and pork recipes are perfect for wraps, stir-fries, or omelets, or on a pizza. For example, leftover pork from this recipe is easily transformed into Basil-Balsamic Wraps: Stir-fry leftover rice and bite-size pieces of pork in a medium skillet over medium-high heat until heated through. Wrap in a flour tortilla and add shredded Cheddar cheese, black beans, chopped scallion, and sour cream. Who says leftovers have to be boring!?

Here's a dish that's simply delicious! You'll find many Cajun spice blends at your local grocery store and online. I make a Tex-Mex variation of this dish also: simply substitute in equal measures bold taco seasoning for the Cajun seasoning, Chipotle Roasted-Tomato Sauce (page 176) for the canned tomatoes, and Green Giant Mexicorn in place of plain corn. —KN

CAJUN BRAISED SKILLET CHOPS

MAKES 2 ENTRÉES, 6 SERVINGS EACH

1 TRAY (6–8 POUNDS, OR 12 CHOPS) BONELESS PORK LOIN CHOPS

1 cup shredded Parmesan cheese (about 3½ ounces)

2 tablespoons black pepper

2 tablespoons Cajun seasoning

3 egg whites, lightly beaten

1⅓ cups chicken broth

1 (15-ounce) can sweet corn, drained

1 (14½-ounce) can petite-cut tomatoes

⅔ cup diced onion

2 tablespoons minced garlic (about 18 cloves)

2 one-gallon freezer bags, labeled

2 one-quart freezer bags

ON HAND FOR COOKING EACH ENTRÉE

1½ tablespoons vegetable oil

1. Rinse and trim chops as desired.

2. Lay out two shallow dishes. Put the egg whites in one dish. Mix the Parmesan, pepper, and Cajun seasoning in the other. Dip the chops into the egg, then dredge in Parmesan coating.

3. Place each chop onto a rimmed baking sheet. When all chops are coated, place in the freezer for 1 hour. Discard remaining egg and Parmesan mixture.

4. Into each 1-quart freezer bag measure ⅔ cup chicken broth, ⅔ cup corn, ⅔ cup tomatoes, ⅓ cup onion, and 1 tablespoon garlic. Seal.

5. Divide frozen chops evenly among the 1-gallon freezer bags. Place one bag tomato mixture into each bag of chops.

6. Seal and freeze.

TO COOK ONE ENTRÉE

1. Completely thaw one entrée in the refrigerator.

2. Heat oil in a deep skillet or Dutch oven over medium heat. Fry chops 3 minutes on each side; remove from the pan.

3. Pour broth and vegetables into pan. Gently scrape browned bits from the bottom; reduce heat to medium-low. Return chops to pan. Simmer, covered, 15 to 20 minutes, turning chops occasionally, or until an instant-read thermometer inserted into the thickest part of a chop reads 160°F.

CREOLE, CAJUN, OR ACADIAN?

After the Gulf of Mexico hurricanes of 2005 I became interested in the region's food traditions. I began exploring the differences among Creole, Cajun, and Acadian cooking. Based on the heavier use of pungent spices in this recipe, this dish likely leans toward Cajun.

A favorite of many clients and friends, this recipe began in the kitchen of our friend Shawnee. She says, "Enjoy this south-of-the-border flavor without a south-of-the-border morning headache." —KN / LT

MARGARITA PORK CHOPS

MAKES 3 ENTRÉES, 4 SERVINGS EACH

1 TRAY (6–8 POUNDS, OR 12 CHOPS) PORK LOIN CHOPS, BONELESS OR BONE-IN

4½ cups bottled margarita mix

6 tablespoons minced garlic (about 54 cloves)

6 teaspoons salt

3 teaspoons black pepper

3 one-gallon freezer bags, labeled

1. Rinse and divide chops evenly among the freezer bags.

2. Into each bag measure 1½ cups margarita mix, 2 tablespoons garlic, 2 teaspoons salt, and 1 teaspoon pepper.

3. Seal and freeze.

THICK AND THIN

Warehouse packages of boneless pork loin chops can vary in size quite a bit. Sometimes packages contain as few as 9 chops, while other times a full dozen. Sometimes I mix and match chop sizes to even out these differences. For example, if packages contain nine 1-inch thick chops, I divide six of these chops among the bags. The remaining three are cut in half lengthwise to yield six thin chops, which are also added to the marinade. The larger chops are for adults; the smaller ones for kids. Varying portion sizes to accommodate different appetites helps stretch the budget, too! —KN

TO COOK ONE ENTRÉE

Prepare on an outdoor grill or indoors under a broiler.

1. Completely thaw one entrée in the refrigerator.

FOR OUTDOOR COOKING

1. Prepare a medium fire in a gas or charcoal grill.

2. Cook chops, turning occasionally, until an instant-read thermometer inserted into the thickest part of a chop reads 160°F. Baste the chops as desired. Do not baste during final 5 minutes of cooking. Discard remaining marinade.

FOR INDOOR COOKING

Arrange chops on a greased broiler pan. Broil chops under high heat 5 inches from the heat source, turning frequently, for 14 to 18 minutes, or until an instant-read thermometer inserted into the thickest part of a chop reads 160°F. Baste the chops as desired. Do not baste during final 5 minutes of cooking. Discard remaining marinade.

The beautiful yellow marinade in this dish mellows once grilled, leaving just the right amount of flavor and a golden color. Try serving your pork chops with hash browns, applesauce, and sour cream — the perfect flavor combination. —LT

MUSTARD-OREGANO CHOPS

MAKES 3 ENTRÉES, 4 SERVINGS EACH

1 TRAY (6–8 POUNDS, OR 12 CHOPS) PORK LOIN CHOPS, BONELESS OR BONE-IN

½ cup prepared mustard

¼ cup red wine vinegar

¼ cup lemon juice

¼ cup vegetable oil

2 tablespoons honey

3 teaspoons dried oregano

3 teaspoons minced garlic (about 9 cloves)

3 one-gallon freezer bags, labeled

1. Rinse and divide chops evenly among the freezer bags.

2. Whisk together mustard, vinegar, lemon juice, oil, and honey in a medium bowl. Divide the marinade evenly over the chops. Into each bag measure 1 teaspoon oregano and 1 teaspoon garlic.

3. Seal and freeze.

RED WINE VINEGAR

The gallon jug of red wine vinegar at the warehouse clubs is a fantastic value, costing 8 to 10 times less per fluid ounce than that found in the grocery store. According to the Vinegar Institute, vinegar will keep almost indefinitely if stored in a cool, dark place. If you are tight on storage space, consider sharing the jug with friends or family.

TO COOK ONE ENTRÉE

Prepare on an outdoor grill or indoors under a broiler.

1. Completely thaw one entrée in the refrigerator.

FOR OUTDOOR COOKING

1. Prepare a medium fire in a gas or charcoal grill.

2. Cook chops, turning occasionally, until an instant-read thermometer inserted into the thickest part of a chop reads 160°F. Baste the chops as desired. Do not baste during final 5 minutes of cooking. Discard remaining marinade.

FOR INDOOR COOKING

Arrange chops on a greased broiler pan. Broil chops under high heat 5 inches from the heat source, turning frequently, for 15 to 18 minutes, or until an instant-read thermometer inserted into the thickest part of a chop reads 160°F. Baste the chops as desired. Do not baste during final 5 minutes of cooking. Discard remaining marinade.

When I moved back to the Portland metropolitan area, one of my first shopping excursions was to Penzeys spice store on the other side of town. It was early in the day and I had time to chat with the clerk, smell spices, and talk about cooking. I told her I was hoping to try a more exotic blend of spices from the Middle East, and she recommended their Turkish blend. If the Penzeys Turkish spice blend isn't easily available, you can try our handmade version below — it doesn't contain sumac like theirs does, but it still makes a mighty tasty chop. —KN

TURKISH PORK LOIN CHOPS
WITH BACON

MAKES 2 ENTRÉES, 5–6 SERVINGS EACH

1 TRAY (6–8 POUNDS, OR 12 CHOPS) BONELESS PORK LOIN CHOPS

¼ cup Turkish seasoning (try our handmade version on the following page)

12–15 slices bacon

15–20 toothpicks

2 one-gallon freezer bags, labeled

1. Rinse and trim chops as desired.

2. Rub 1 teaspoon of Turkish seasoning over the surfaces of each chop. Wrap one or more slices of bacon around the edge of each chop, securing with toothpicks.

3. Place wrapped chops on a rimmed baking sheet and place in the freezer for 1 hour. Divide frozen chops evenly among the freezer bags. To avoid puncturing the bags, you might wish to double-bag the chops.

4. Seal and return to the freezer.

TO COOK ONE ENTRÉE

1. Place chops in an ungreased baking dish. Cover and completely thaw in the refrigerator.

2. Preheat the oven to 350°F.

3. Bake chops, uncovered, for 45 to 60 minutes, or until an instant-read thermometer inserted into the thickest part of a chop reads 160°F.

HANDMADE TURKISH SEASONING

Make your own seasoning by mixing together the following spices:

1 tablespoon salt, 1 tablespoon garlic granules, 1 tablespoon ground cumin, 2 teaspoons black pepper, 2 teaspoons dried oregano, 1 teaspoon dried cilantro, ½ teaspoon cayenne pepper

BAKING DISH SIZES

Two to four chops will fit nicely in a 9- by 9-inch baking dish. If cooking five or more chops, use a 13- by 9-inch baking dish.

A number of years ago, my friend Tamara sent me a homemade cookbook for my birthday. It was filled with all her favorite recipes and penned in her own funky handwriting. It's one of the best gifts I've ever received. Unlike many of the cookbooks I own that have provided me with one or two good recipes, Tamara's is chock-full of great ones. This one, named for her friend Cam, has been changed a bit to reflect my own tastes, but it retains its original name. —LT

CAM'S RIBS

MAKES 3 ENTRÉES, 6 SERVINGS EACH

1 TRAY (ABOUT 9 POUNDS) BONELESS COUNTRY-STYLE RIBS

3 cups ketchup

1½ cups red wine vinegar

1½ cups Worcestershire sauce

1½ cups packed brown sugar

1½ tablespoons minced garlic (about 14 cloves)

1½ tablespoons minced onion

1½ tablespoons dry mustard

1½ teaspoons black pepper

3 one-gallon freezer bags, labeled

3 one-quart freezer bags

1. Divide ribs evenly among the 1-gallon freezer bags.

2. Whisk together ketchup, vinegar, Worcestershire sauce, brown sugar, garlic, onion, mustard, and pepper in a large bowl. Divide the sauce evenly among the 1-quart freezer bags. Note in this recipe the sauce is kept separate from the meat. Seal.

3. Place a bag of sauce into each bag of ribs. Seal and freeze.

TO COOK ONE ENTRÉE

1. Completely thaw one entrée in the refrigerator. Place the ribs in a large stockpot and cover with water. Set bag of sauce aside.

2. Simmer ribs about 1 hour, or until tender. Preheat the oven to 350°F.

3. Drain ribs and place in an ungreased baking dish. Pour sauce over ribs.

4. Bake, uncovered, basting ribs with sauce every 10 minutes, for 1 hour.

BUYING TIPS

Packages of country-style ribs vary in size by several pounds. Buy as close to 9 pounds as possible, or, alternatively, in multiples of 3 and make more or less sauce accordingly. Because you're measuring sauce ingredients into each bag separately, you can easily alter the number of entrées you make.

The original version of this dish, and a lot of my cooking knowledge, came from my mom. The aroma that fills the house when these ribs are baking is terrific. —LT

STICKY RIBS

MAKES 3 ENTRÉES, 6 SERVINGS EACH

1 TRAY (ABOUT 9 POUNDS) BONELESS COUNTRY-STYLE RIBS

2¼ cups packed brown sugar

3 cups water

¾ cup soy sauce

3 tablespoons minced garlic (about 27 cloves)

3 one-gallon freezer bags, labeled

3 one-quart freezer bags

1. Divide ribs evenly among the 1-gallon freezer bags.

2. Into each 1-quart freezer bag, measure ¾ cup brown sugar, 1 cup water, ¼ cup soy sauce, and 1 tablespoon garlic. Note in this recipe the sauce is kept separate from the meat. Seal.

3. Place a bag of sauce into each bag of ribs. Seal and freeze.

TO COOK ONE ENTRÉE

1. Completely thaw one entrée in the refrigerator.

2. Place the ribs in a large stockpot and cover with water. Set bag of sauce aside.

3. Simmer ribs about 1 hour, or until tender. Preheat the oven to 350°F.

4. Drain ribs and place in an ungreased baking dish. Pour sauce over ribs. Bake, uncovered, for about 1 hour, or until sauce is thick and sticky.

Here's a tangy dish that's just a bit spicy. If you prefer your food less spicy, reduce the amount of crushed red pepper or jalapeño pepper sauce. If you want the meat less tangy, replace ⅔–1 cup of the cider vinegar with an equal amount of chicken broth. —KN

FIREHOUSE PORK SKEWERS

MAKES 3 ENTRÉES, 6 SERVINGS EACH

1 TRAY (ABOUT 4½ POUNDS) PORK TENDERLOIN

2 cups cider vinegar

1½ tablespoons jalapeño hot sauce

1 tablespoon Worcestershire sauce

1 tablespoon soy sauce

1½ teaspoons black pepper

1½ teaspoons crushed red pepper flakes

1½ cups chopped onion (about 1 large)

3 one-gallon freezer bags, labeled

ON HAND FOR COOKING EACH ENTRÉE

1 medium onion, cut into 8 wedges

10–12 (9-inch) wooden or metal skewers

1. Rinse and trim tenderloin as desired. Cut pork into 1-inch cubes. Divide evenly among the freezer bags.

2. Mix vinegar, hot sauce, Worcestershire sauce, and soy sauce in a medium bowl. Divide marinade evenly over the pork. Into each bag measure ½ teaspoon black pepper, ½ teaspoon crushed red pepper, and ½ cup onion.

3. Seal and freeze.

TO COOK ONE ENTRÉE

1. Completely thaw one entrée in the refrigerator.

2. Prepare a medium fire in a gas or charcoal grill.

3. If using wooden skewers, soak them in water while meat is thawing. Thread pork pieces and onion onto skewers. Grill 12 to 15 minutes, turning occasionally, until thoroughly cooked. Discard remaining marinade.

This is such a tasty dish, you'll be tempted to have it on hand throughout the year. I make this entrée often because the children like it so much. To keep things interesting, I might cut the meat into cubes for kabobs and then finish the recipe as directed. Then after thawing, I alternate the pork pieces with pineapple, mango, or steamed sweet potato and head for the grill. Whether whole or in kabobs, this is a versatile, delicious dish! —KN

CARIBBEAN PORK TENDERLOIN

MAKES 3 ENTRÉES, 6 SERVINGS EACH

1 TRAY (ABOUT 4½ POUNDS) PORK TENDERLOIN

⅓ cup white vinegar

3 tablespoons packed brown sugar

3 tablespoons soy sauce

3 teaspoons dried thyme

3 teaspoons ground allspice

3 teaspoons salt

¾ teaspoon black pepper

¾ teaspoon ground cinnamon

18 scallions, chopped
(about 3 cups)

1½ cups chopped onion
(about 1 large)

3 tablespoons minced ginger

3 teaspoons minced garlic
(about 9 cloves)

3 one-gallon freezer bags, labeled

ON HAND FOR COOKING EACH ENTRÉE

Vegetable cooking spray

1. Rinse and trim tenderloin as desired. Place 1½ pounds pork (or one-third of the meat) into each freezer bag.

2. Mix vinegar, sugar, and soy sauce in a large bowl. Divide the marinade evenly over the pork. Into each bag measure 1 teaspoon thyme, 1 teaspoon allspice, 1 teaspoon salt, ¼ teaspoon pepper, and ¼ teaspoon cinnamon. Gently shake each bag to distribute spices. Into each bag measure 1 cup scallions, ½ cup onion, 1 tablespoon ginger, and 1 teaspoon garlic.

3. Seal and freeze.

TO COOK ONE ENTRÉE

1. Completely thaw one entrée in the refrigerator.

2. Prepare a medium-low fire in a gas or charcoal grill.

3. Lightly coat grill rack with cooking spray. Grill tenderloin until an instant-read thermometer inserted into the thickest part of the pork reads 160°F. Discard remaining marinade.

BROWN SUGAR

Many pantry staples such as brown sugar can be purchased at the warehouse club for half the price you would find at the grocery store. Keep unused portions of brown sugar in the freezer to prevent hardening and loss of flavor.

This is the ultimate autumn dish! When everyone arrives home from a busy day and the sun has already gone down, the comforting aroma of simmered apples drifts from the oven and lifts your spirits. —KN / LT

APPLE AND CRANBERRY PORK LOIN

MAKES 3 ENTRÉES, 6–8 SERVINGS EACH

1 PORK LOIN (ABOUT 8 POUNDS; DO NOT USE TIED PORK LOIN ROAST)

6 medium tart apples, peeled, cored, and sliced (about 8 cups)

⅔ cup apple jelly

3 cups diced onion (about 3 medium)

¾ cup dried cranberries

3 tablespoons cider vinegar

3 teaspoons dry mustard

3 one-gallon freezer bags, labeled

1. Rinse and trim loin as desired. Cut pork into three equal roasts. Place one roast into each freezer bag.

2. Divide apple slices and apple jelly evenly over the roasts. Into each bag measure 1 cup onion, ¼ cup cranberries, 1 tablespoon vinegar, and 1 teaspoon mustard.

3. Seal and freeze.

TO COOK ONE ENTRÉE

1. Completely thaw one entrée in the refrigerator.

2. Preheat the oven to 350°F.

3. Place roast in the center of an ungreased baking dish, distributing apples and onions around the meat. Bake, uncovered, for 1 hour, or until an instant-read thermometer inserted into the thickest part of the roast reads 160°F.

APPLE JELLY

The apple jelly for this recipe is commonly found in 10-ounce and 18-ounce jars. If you buy the 10-ounce jar, you can use it all without measuring.

This recipe is the happy result of several brains working together. I found the sausages and came up with the initial concept, my friends Shawnee and Mike worked on it, and a star was born. The sauce makes this dish special. —KN

PORK LOIN
WITH APRICOT/SAUSAGE STUFFING

MAKES 3 ENTRÉES, 6–8 SERVINGS EACH

1 PORK LOIN (ABOUT 8 POUNDS; DO NOT USE TIED PORK LOIN ROAST)

1½ cups dried apricots, chopped

6 links chicken-apple sausage (such as Aidells), diced

¾ cup diced onion (about 1 small)

¾ cup Dijon mustard

¾ cup honey

3 one-gallon freezer bags, labeled

6 one-quart freezer bags

ON HAND FOR COOKING EACH ENTRÉE

¼ cup sour cream

1. Rinse and trim loin as desired. Cut loin into three equal roasts. With one hand held flat across the top of each roast, use a sharp knife to cut a pocket in the middle of the pork. Take care to cut up to but not through the end of the roast, and leave the sides intact. (The pockets will be stuffed later.) Place one roast into each 1-gallon bag.

2. Combine apricots, sausages, and onion in a medium bowl; divide evenly among three of the 1-quart bags. Seal.

3. Mix the mustard and honey in a medium bowl; divide evenly among the remaining 1-quart bags. Seal.

4. Place a bag of stuffing and a bag of sauce directly into each bag with roast. Seal and freeze.

TO COOK ONE ENTRÉE

1. Completely thaw one entrée in the refrigerator. Stuff roast pocket with the apricot and sausage mixture.

2. Preheat the oven to 350°F.

3. Place roast in an ungreased baking dish. Spread sauce over the roast, covering completely. Bake, uncovered, for 45 to 60 minutes, or until an instant-read thermometer inserted into the stuffing and the thickest part of the roast reads 160°F.

4. When roast is done, transfer drippings to a small saucepan and simmer until liquid reduces by about half. Stir in ¼ cup sour cream and spoon over pork slices.

SMALL FREEZER BAGS

One-pint freezer bags are great for holding smaller portions, such as the mustard sauce for this recipe. While most warehouse clubs do not carry pint-size bags, they can be found at the grocery store and used in place of the quart-size bags in many of our recipes.

My husband's father and stepmother were born and raised in Austria. They're excellent models of living simply and sensibly, making every dollar count while still enjoying life to the fullest. Anything my mother-in-law makes immediately becomes a family favorite — she's an excellent cook! —LT

AUSTRIAN PORK GOULASH

MAKES 3 ENTRÉES, 6 SERVINGS EACH

1 PORK LOIN (ABOUT 8 POUNDS; DO NOT USE TIED PORK LOIN ROAST)

¼ cup vegetable oil

5 pounds onions, chopped

1 cup water

¼ cup beef bouillon granules

¼ cup minced garlic (about 36 cloves)

3 tablespoons dried thyme

2 tablespoons paprika

2 teaspoons salt

2 teaspoons black pepper

3 one-gallon freezer bags, labeled

1. Rinse and trim loin as desired. Cut pork into small cubes, removing all visible fat. Divide evenly among the freezer bags.

2. Heat oil in a large stockpot over medium heat. Add onions and cook, stirring occasionally, until soft, about 15 minutes. Add water and stir. Add bouillon, garlic, thyme, paprika, salt, and pepper. Cook, stirring occasionally, for 10 minutes longer. Cool.

3. Divide cooled onion mixture evenly over the pork.

4. Seal and freeze.

TO COOK ONE ENTRÉE

1. Completely thaw one entrée in the refrigerator.

2. Put pork and onion mixture in a large stockpot and add 1½ cups water. Cook goulash over medium heat until pork is completely cooked through and sauce has thickened, 30 to 40 minutes. Add more water during cooking if goulash becomes dry. Serve over hot rice.

CLASSIC FAVORITES

Traditional family favorites such as goulash and hash may seem old-fashioned, but you'll be surprised at how our updates give these authentic recipes modern appeal.

Simmered in the slow cooker all day, this zesty roast shreds easily with a fork. Serve it over pasta or cheese ravioli. Or cook and shred one roast to make two pans of the Pork Ragout Lasagna on the next page. —KN

PORK LOIN RAGOUT

MAKES 3 ENTRÉES, 6–8 SERVINGS EACH

1 PORK LOIN (ABOUT 8 POUNDS; DO NOT USE TIED PORK LOIN ROAST)

1 tablespoon dried oregano

1 tablespoon dried basil

2 tablespoons granulated garlic

½ teaspoon salt

½ teaspoon black pepper

9 cups (72 ounces) marinara sauce (try our Basic Red Sauce on page 178)

6 tablespoons balsamic or red wine vinegar

6 bay leaves

2 large onions, coarsely chopped

2 large green bell peppers, coarsely chopped

6 one-gallon freezer bags, label 3

3 one-quart freezer bags

1. Mix oregano, basil, garlic, salt, and black pepper in a small bowl and set aside.

2. Rinse and trim loin as desired. Cut loin into three equal roasts. Rub each roast with one-third of the oregano seasoning mixture. Place one roast into each unlabeled 1-gallon bag.

3. Over each roast, measure 3 cups marinara sauce, 2 tablespoons vinegar, and 2 bay leaves. Seal bag.

4. Divide the onion and pepper pieces evenly among the 1-quart bags. Seal. Place a bag of pork and sauce and a bag of peppers and onions into each labeled 1-gallon bag.

5. Seal and freeze.

TO COOK ONE ENTRÉE

1. Completely thaw one entrée in the refrigerator.

2. Put onion and pepper mixture into slow cooker. Put roast and sauce on top. Cook on low for 8 to 10 hours.

3. Remove bay leaves. Shred cooked pork with a fork, mix with the sauce, and serve over pasta.

This recipe is my variation of Lindsay's Classic Lasagna recipe. She sent her original recipes with a brief note: "Work your magic with the ragout . . . " You'll notice I call for more noodles than Lindsay does in the original recipe. My pans are large, so it takes more to cover the bottom. You should use the number of noodles required to cover the bottom of your pan in a single layer with no overlap. —KN

PORK RAGOUT LASAGNA

MAKES 2 ENTRÉES, 12 SERVINGS EACH

1 BAG PORK LOIN RAGOUT (PAGE 133)

8 cups Basic Red Sauce (page 178)

1 (48-ounce) container cottage cheese (6 cups)

4 eggs, lightly beaten

2½ cups shredded Asiago cheese, divided into 2 cups and ½ cup

18–24 lasagna noodles, uncooked

6½ cups shredded mozzarella cheese

Two 13- by 9- by 2-inch baking dishes

Plastic wrap

Aluminum foil

1. Cook Pork Loin Ragout according to directions on page 133. Remove the roast from the slow cooker and shred with a fork. Remove and discard bay leaves. Pour sauce into a large bowl. Add shredded pork and red sauce; mix well and set aside.

2. In a separate large bowl, mix cottage cheese, eggs, and 2 cups of the Asiago. Lay baking dishes before you and assemble both lasagnas at once in layers in the following order:

LAYER 1

4 uncooked noodles

2 cups pork sauce

2 cups cottage cheese mixture

1 cup mozzarella

LAYER 2

4 uncooked noodles

2 cups pork sauce

2 cups cottage cheese mixture – or whatever remains

1 cup mozzarella

LAYER 3

4 uncooked noodles

2 cups pork sauce – or whatever remains

1¼ cups mozzarella

¼ cup Asiago

3. Wrap each dish entirely in plastic wrap. Top with foil, label, and freeze.

TO COOK ONE ENTRÉE

1. Completely thaw one entrée in the refrigerator.

2. Preheat the oven to 375°F.

3. Remove plastic wrap and foil from baking dish and replace foil. Bake for 50 minutes. Remove foil and continue baking 20 to 30 minutes longer, or until center is hot and the cheeses are browned. Remove from oven and let stand for 10 minutes before serving.

NOTE: This lasagna can be cooked without freezing; however, allow it to sit in the refrigerator for a day or more so that the noodles absorb liquid and soften before baking.

Years ago my husband's employer asked him keep a little journal to record his ideas while at work. Apparently this is something engineers do frequently as backup evidence of patentable ideas. At first I teased him, but later I realized that I needed to carry one also! Not because my ideas are patentable but because I have such trouble remembering things. Now, whenever I think of a new flavor combination (such as the cake spice in this recipe) or sample a magnificent restaurant dish, I have my little book on hand to take notes. —KN

HONEY AND SPICE PORK KABOBS

MAKES 3 ENTRÉES, 6–8 SERVINGS EACH

1 PORK LOIN (ABOUT 8 POUNDS; DO NOT USE TIED PORK LOIN ROAST)

3 cups orange juice

1½ cups honey

1 tablespoon cake spice (such as Penzeys, or try our handmade version below)

1½ teaspoons salt

3 teaspoons minced garlic (about 9 cloves)

3 one-gallon freezer bags, labeled

ON HAND FOR COOKING EACH ENTRÉE

10–12 (9-inch) wooden or metal skewers

1. Rinse and trim loin as desired. Cut pork into 1-inch cubes; divide evenly among the freezer bags.

2. Whisk together orange juice, honey, cake spice, and salt in a medium bowl. Divide the marinade evenly over the pork. Into each bag measure 1 teaspoon minced garlic.

3. Seal and freeze.

HANDMADE CAKE SPICE

Make your own seasoning by mixing together the following spices:

1 teaspoon ground cinnamon, ½ teaspoon ground anise, ½ teaspoon ground nutmeg, ½ teaspoon ground allspice, ½ teaspoon ground ginger, ½ teaspoon ground cloves

Use the whole amount in the Honey and Spice Pork Kabobs, or as you like in your favorite baked dishes.

TO COOK ONE ENTRÉE

1. Completely thaw one entrée in the refrigerator. If using wooden skewers, soak them in water while meat is thawing.

2. Prepare a medium-low fire in a gas or charcoal grill.

3. Thread pork pieces onto skewers. Grill, turning occasionally and basting as desired, 15 to 18 minutes until thoroughly cooked. Do not baste during final 5 minutes of cooking. Discard remaining marinade.

When I have trouble thinking of something to make for company, I often return to this favorite. The recipe is just as delicious with chicken breast or a tender cut of beef such as sirloin. My family regularly enjoys brown rice, but they insist that this dish is better with white. Steamed vegetables complete the meal. —LT

RAGING GARLIC PORK STIR-FRY

MAKES 4 ENTRÉES, 4–6 SERVINGS EACH

1 PORK LOIN (ABOUT 8 POUNDS; DO NOT USE TIED PORK LOIN ROAST)

1½ cups soy sauce

½ cup white wine vinegar

2 tablespoons sugar

8 teaspoons minced garlic (about 24 cloves)

1 teaspoon (or to taste) crushed red pepper flakes

4 large onions, cut into 2-inch pieces

4 large green bell peppers, cut into 2-inch pieces

4 one-gallon freezer bags, labeled

12 one-quart freezer bags

ON HAND FOR COOKING EACH ENTRÉE

2 teaspoons vegetable oil

½ cup cornstarch

1. Rinse and trim loin as desired. Cut pork into bite-size cubes; divide evenly among four of the 1-quart bags. Seal.

2. Whisk together soy sauce, vinegar, and sugar in a medium bowl. Divide the marinade evenly among four 1-quart bags. Into each bag of sauce measure 2 teaspoons garlic and ¼ teaspoon crushed red pepper. Seal.

3. Divide onions and bell peppers evenly among the remaining 1-quart bags. Seal.

4. Into each of the 1-gallon bags, place a bag of pork, a bag of sauce, and a bag of peppers and onions. Seal and freeze.

TO COOK ONE ENTRÉE

1. Completely thaw one entrée in the refrigerator.

2. Pour off and discard any accumulated liquid from the bag of pork. Add ½ cup cornstarch; seal bag and shake to coat the meat.

3. Heat oil in a large skillet over medium-high heat. Add pork and stir-fry until thoroughly cooked, about 10 minutes. Add vegetables and sauce. Stir-fry just until vegetables are tender crisp.

Honey and bourbon are the main attractions in this sassy dinner production. Clearly not a coat-and-tie dish, it's great for a casual cookout with family and friends. This recipe makes ample marinade for a pork loin weighing up to 9 pounds. —KN

STICKY DRUNK PIG ON A STICK

MAKES 3 ENTRÉES, 6–8 SERVINGS EACH

1 PORK LOIN (ABOUT 8 POUNDS; DO NOT USE TIED PORK LOIN ROAST)

1½ cups bourbon

1½ cups soy sauce

1½ cups lemon juice

1½ cups honey

3 tablespoons olive oil

1½ cups chopped onion (about 1 large)

3 tablespoons minced ginger

3 teaspoons minced garlic (about 9 cloves)

¾ teaspoon black pepper

3 one-gallon freezer bags, labeled

ON HAND FOR COOKING EACH ENTRÉE

10–12 (9-inch) wooden or metal skewers

1. Rinse and trim loin as desired. Cut pork into 1-inch cubes; divide evenly among freezer bags.

2. Whisk bourbon, soy sauce, lemon juice, honey, and oil in a medium bowl. Divide the marinade evenly over the pork. Into each bag measure ½ cup onion, 1 tablespoon ginger, 1 teaspoon garlic, and ¼ teaspoon pepper.

3. Seal and freeze.

TO COOK ONE ENTRÉE

1. Completely thaw one entrée in the refrigerator. If using wooden skewers, soak them in water while meat is thawing.

2. Prepare a medium-low fire in a gas or charcoal grill.

3. Thread pork pieces onto skewers. Cook 15 to 18 minutes, turning occasionally and basting as desired, until thoroughly cooked. Do not baste during final 5 minutes of cooking. Discard remaining marinade.

COMMUNITY COOKING

One of the benefits of participating in a cooking club is sharing costs. Take the bourbon in this recipe. If you had to buy it yourself, you might skip making this dish entirely. But you may be tempted to try it if you're splitting the bill. For more discussion of cooking communities and their benefits, see page 214.

Come home and enjoy this Mediterranean-style roast after a busy day. Slow cooking your main dish leaves you a little extra time for finishing touches: a roasted head of garlic to spread on a fresh baguette, fresh mozzarella over sliced tomatoes topped with fresh basil leaves, or perhaps a simple spinach salad with red onion, pitted Kalamata olives, and feta. —KN

GARLIC-STUDDED PORK LOIN

MAKES 3 ENTRÉES, 6–8 SERVINGS EACH

1 PORK LOIN (ABOUT 8 POUNDS)

2 tablespoons dried oregano

1 tablespoon salt

1 tablespoon black pepper

18 garlic cloves

¾ cup olive oil

¾ cup lemon juice

¾ cup water

3 one-gallon freezer bags, labeled

1. Mix oregano, salt, and pepper in a small bowl and set aside.

2. Rinse and trim loin as desired. Cut loin into three equal roasts. Using the tip of a sharp paring knife, cut twelve openings ¾ inch deep in each roast. Slice each garlic clove in half and place one garlic piece in each opening.

3. Rub each roast with one-third of the seasoning mixture. Place one roast into each freezer bag. Over each roast, measure ¼ cup oil, ¼ cup lemon juice, and ¼ cup water.

4. Seal and freeze.

TO COOK ONE ENTRÉE

Completely thaw one entrée in the refrigerator. Put roast
and marinade in the slow cooker and cook on low for 8
to 10 hours.

LEMON JUICE FROM CONCENTRATE

If you choose bottled lemon juice, take care to check the expiration date
on the bottles. While 2-packs of lemon juice are three to five times less
expensive per fluid ounce at the warehouse club, it does not keep indefinitely. If you purchase more than you will use in cooking, consider using
it to clean around the house. Lemon is a natural cleaning agent and
deodorizer. Contact the manufacturer for other household uses or con-
sult some of the books in our Resources section.

CHAPTER FOUR

MEATLESS MAINS, SIDES, AND SOUPS

All of my testers for this recipe were impressed by the flavors in the simple, versatile marinade for this dish. One container of sauce is appropriate for two grilled mushrooms, as in this recipe, or in the Fresh Vegetable Stir-Fry with Marinated Tofu on the following page. Two mushroom caps divided are a perfect lunch for four. For a dinner entrée, use both containers to marinate four mushroom caps. —KN

ASIAN MARKET MARINADE
FOR PORTOBELLO MUSHROOMS

MAKES 2 MARINADES, FOR 2 PORTOBELLO MUSHROOM CAPS EACH

1 cup Asian-style salad dressing (such as Newman's Own Low Fat Sesame Ginger)

½ cup peanut sauce (such as House of Tsang)

¼ cup lite soy sauce

4 teaspoons toasted sesame oil

½ teaspoon red curry paste or hot chili oil (such as House of Tsang Mongolian Fire Oil)

4 tablespoons chopped scallions

2 small square freezer containers, labeled

ON HAND FOR COOKING EACH ENTRÉE

2 PORTOBELLO MUSHROOM CAPS, CLEANED

Chopped scallions, chopped peanuts, or chopped fresh cilantro for garnish (optional)

1. Whisk together salad dressing, peanut sauce, soy sauce, sesame oil, and curry paste in a small bowl; divide sauce evenly between the freezer containers. Into each container, measure 2 tablespoons scallions.

2. Seal and freeze.

TO USE THE MARINADE WITH FRESH PORTOBELLOS

1. Completely thaw one marinade in the refrigerator.

2. Marinate mushroom caps for 1 hour.

3. Prepare a medium-low fire in a gas or charcoal grill.

4. Grill 6 to 8 minutes per side, or until tender. Slice and serve over rice or noodles. Garnish with scallions, peanuts, or cilantro, if desired.

This dish is full of fiber plus important vitamins and minerals such as vitamin A, vitamin C, potassium, and folic acid. Many of the vegetables are available at farmers' markets during the growing season. Farmers' markets are fun for the whole family and a great way to support your local growers. If your family doesn't like tofu, omit it and enjoy the vegetables and Asian flavors. —KN

FRESH VEGETABLE STIR-FRY
WITH ASIAN MARINATED TOFU

MAKES 1 ENTRÉE, 6–8 SERVINGS

1 CONTAINER ASIAN MARKET MARINADE (PAGE 144)

1 pound extra-firm tofu, cut into 1-inch pieces

1 teaspoon sesame oil

2 cups broccoli florets (about 5 ounces)

1 cup green beans, cut into 1-inch pieces (about 4 ounces)

1 cup chopped scallions

1 cup sliced carrots (about 2 medium)

5 ounces soba noodles, cooked and drained

½ cup peanuts, chopped (optional)

1. Completely thaw marinade in the refrigerator.

2. Gently stir marinade to recombine and set aside ¼ cup.

3. Put tofu in a medium bowl. Pour remaining marinade over tofu; mix to coat. Marinate in refrigerator for 1 to 2 hours, stirring occasionally. Drain marinade from tofu.

4. Heat oil over medium-high heat in a wok. Add tofu and cook, stirring, until lightly browned, 4 to 5 minutes. Add broccoli, green beans, scallions, and carrots. Cook, stirring, until vegetables are tender crisp, 4 to 5 minutes. Add reserved marinade and noodles and cook until heated through.

5. Serve over rice. Garnish with peanuts, if desired.

When light fare or a vegetarian entrée is in order, portobello mushrooms fill the bill. —LT

CAESAR PORTOBELLO MUSHROOMS

MAKES 2 MARINADES, FOR 2 PORTOBELLO MUSHROOM CAPS EACH

¾ cup olive oil

¼ cup white wine vinegar

¼ cup lemon juice

2 teaspoons Dijon mustard

½ teaspoon salt

2 teaspoons minced garlic
(about 6 cloves)

½ teaspoon black pepper

*2 small square freezer containers,
labeled*

ON HAND FOR COOKING EACH ENTRÉE

**2 PORTOBELLO MUSHROOM
CAPS, CLEANED**

¼ cup shredded Parmesan cheese

1. Whisk together oil, vinegar, lemon juice, mustard, and salt in a small bowl. Divide marinade evenly between the freezer containers. Into each container, measure 1 teaspoon garlic and ¼ teaspoon pepper.

2. Seal and freeze.

PORTOBELLO MUSHROOMS

Portobellos have gained popularity over the last several years. They're sometimes referred to as "steak mushrooms" because of their size and suitability for marinating and grilling.

TO COOK ONE ENTRÉE

This entrée can be prepared outdoors on a grill or in the kitchen using your broiler.

1. Completely thaw one marinade in the refrigerator.

2. Marinate mushroom caps for 1 hour.

FOR OUTDOOR COOKING

1. Prepare a medium fire in a gas or charcoal grill.

2. Grill, turning occasionally, 10 to 12 minutes, or until tender. Fill the inside of each mushroom cap with 2 tablespoons Parmesan and grill until melted.

FOR INDOOR COOKING

Arrange mushrooms on an ungreased broiler pan. Broil under high heat, 5 inches from the heat source, for about 2 minutes on each side. Fill the inside of each mushroom cap with 2 tablespoons Parmesan and broil until melted.

These grilled mushrooms team up nicely with polenta or couscous. —LT

MAPLE PORTOBELLO MUSHROOMS

MAKES 2 MARINADES, FOR 2 PORTOBELLO MUSHROOM CAPS EACH

½ cup maple syrup

½ cup olive oil

¼ cup lemon juice

2 tablespoons spicy brown mustard

1 teaspoon salt

4 teaspoons minced garlic

1 teaspoon dried thyme

1 teaspoon black pepper

2 small square freezer containers, labeled

ON HAND FOR COOKING EACH ENTRÉE

2 PORTOBELLO MUSHROOM CAPS, CLEANED

1. Whisk together maple syrup, oil, lemon juice, mustard, and salt in a medium bowl. Divide the marinade evenly between the freezer containers. Into each container, measure 2 teaspoons garlic, ½ teaspoon thyme, and ½ teaspoon pepper.

2. Seal and freeze.

OLIVE OIL

Warehouse club brand items are developing a positive reputation as quality products offered at a lower price than name brands. My warehouse club's store brand extra-virgin olive oil is two to three times less expensive per ounce than even the least expensive brand at the grocery store. Extra-virgin olive oil is from the first pressing of olives and is the finest olive oil one can buy. Keep your bottle tightly sealed and stored away from heat and light.

TO COOK ONE ENTRÉE

This entrée can be prepared outdoors on a grill or in the kitchen using your boiler.

1. Completely thaw one marinade in the refrigerator.

2. Marinate mushroom caps for 1 hour.

FOR OUTDOOR COOKING

1. Prepare a medium fire in a gas or charcoal grill.

2. Grill mushrooms, turning occasionally, for 10 to 12 minutes, or until tender.

FOR INDOOR COOKING

Arrange mushrooms on a greased broiler pan. Broil under high heat, 5 inches from the heat source, for about 2 minutes on each side.

This hot dish makes an ideal breakfast or brunch for company. It can also be served as a delicious light dinner. —LT

ASPARAGUS AND POTATO FRITTATA

MAKES 3 ENTRÉES, 6–8 SERVINGS EACH

2 POUNDS FRESH ASPARAGUS, CLEANED AND FIBROUS ENDS SNAPPED OFF

3 pounds yellow-flesh potatoes, boiled and cut into bite-size pieces

1 cup chopped onion (about 1 medium)

18 eggs

1½ cups heavy cream

1½ teaspoons salt

¾ teaspoon black pepper

3 one-gallon freezer bags, labeled

1. Place asparagus in a large shallow pan with just enough water to cover. Bring to a boil. Reduce heat and simmer for 2 minutes. Plunge asparagus into cold water to cool quickly. Cut asparagus into bite-size pieces. Divide asparagus, potato, and onion among the freezer bags.

2. Lightly beat six eggs in a medium bowl. Add ½ cup cream, ½ teaspoon salt, and ¼ teaspoon pepper. Pour into one freezer bag and seal. Repeat for the two remaining frittatas.

3. Freeze.

TO COOK ONE ENTRÉE

1. Completely thaw one entrée in the refrigerator.

2. Preheat the oven to 425°F.

3. Pour frittata into a lightly greased 8- by 8-inch baking dish. Bake for 30 minutes, or until egg is cooked through and top is golden brown.

This quick and tasty side dish is a welcome change from plain rice. Pair it with any of our grilled beef, chicken, or pork entrées. —LT

RICE PILAF

MAKES 4 SIDE DISHES, 4–6 SERVINGS EACH

¼ cup olive oil

2 tablespoons butter

6 cups white rice, uncooked

2 cups chopped carrots
(about 4 medium)

1 cup chopped celery
(about 4 stalks)

1 cup chopped onion
(about 1 medium)

8 teaspoons chicken bouillon
granules

4 teaspoons dried parsley

1 teaspoon black pepper

4 one-gallon freezer bags, labeled

1. Heat olive oil and butter in large skillet over medium heat. Add rice, carrots, celery, and onion; cook, stirring, until rice is golden brown, 5 to 7 minutes. Cool.

2. Divide rice mixture among the freezer bags. Into each bag, measure 2 teaspoons bouillon, 1 teaspoon parsley, and ¼ teaspoon pepper.

3. Seal and freeze.

TO COOK ONE SIDE DISH

Place frozen pilaf in a medium saucepan and add 3 cups of water. Bring to a boil; reduce heat and cook, covered, for 20 minutes, or until water is completely absorbed.

If you're looking for an interesting variation on the usual pan lasagna, these rolls will be a treat! Each noodle takes a heaping ⅛ cup of filling (about 3 tablespoons) and is then rolled instead of being layered in a pan. This dish is great for small and large families alike because you can pull out just the right number of rolls to cook for lunch on those busy weekend days. Look for the feta, ricotta, and cottage cheeses at your warehouse club. —KN

FETA AND SPINACH LASAGNA ROLLS

MAKES 8 ENTRÉES, 6–8 ROLLS EACH

3½ (16-ounce) boxes lasagna noodles (15–18 noodles in each box)

1 (24-ounce) container crumbled feta cheese (about 5 cups)

1 (32-ounce) container low-fat cottage cheese (4 cups)

1 (32-ounce) container part-skim ricotta cheese (3½ cups)

1 cup shredded Asiago cheese (about 4 ounces)

1 cup shredded Parmesan cheese

2 teaspoons black pepper

15 ounces frozen chopped spinach, broken apart and leaves separated

8 one-gallon freezer bags, labeled

ON HAND FOR COOKING EACH ENTRÉE

2 cups marinara sauce (try our Basic Red Sauce on page178)

1 cup shredded mozzarella cheese (about 4 ounces)

Aluminum foil

1. Working in batches, boil noodles until flexible enough to roll but not completely cooked.

2. Meanwhile, mix feta, cottage cheese, ricotta, Asiago, Parmesan, and pepper in a large bowl. Stir in spinach leaves.

3. Place partially cooked noodles on a clean work surface in a single layer (do not overlap).

4. Spread 3 tablespoons filling down the length of each noodle. Roll noodle and place seam side down on a rimmed baking sheet. Place rolls in the freezer for 30 minutes.

5. Divide frozen rolls evenly among freezer bags. Seal and refreeze.

TO COOK ONE ENTRÉE

1. Place lasagna rolls in a greased baking dish. Cover with foil; completely thaw in the refrigerator.

2. Preheat the oven to 350°F.

3. Pour 2 cups marinara over rolls and top with mozzarella; replace foil. Bake for 35 to 40 minutes, or until center is hot and cheese is melted.

RULE OF THUMB

Use a 9-inch square baking dish for up to eight rolls and a 13- by 9-inch baking dish for more than eight rolls. If cooking more than eight rolls, you'll need to increase the amounts for the sauce and mozzarella: for every four lasagna rolls, use 1 cup marinara sauce and ½ cup mozzarella.

I grew up in a city where eating out meant visiting any one of a number of small, family-owned, ethnic restaurants. What a culinary adventure! I never tired of the Mediterranean food served in my favorite Greek restaurant. You'll find feta cheese in the deli section of the grocery store, and phyllo pastry in the frozen-food section. —LT

SPANAKOPITA

MAKES 14–16 INDIVIDUAL PASTRIES

**2½ POUNDS FRESH SPIN-
ACH, RINSED, WITH
WATER STILL CLINGING
TO LEAVES**

2 eggs, lightly beaten

¼ cup lemon juice

¼ cup chopped fresh dill
(or 4 teaspoons dried)

1 teaspoon salt

1 teaspoon black pepper

14–16 sheets phyllo dough

2 tablespoons melted butter

1 cup crumbled feta cheese
(about 5 ounces)

Plastic wrap

2 one-gallon freezer bags, labeled

ON HAND FOR BAKING

2 teaspoons melted butter for each
pastry

1. Wilt spinach in a large stockpot over medium heat. Do not overcook. Drain and cool.

2. Using your hands, squeeze as much water from spinach as possible. Place spinach in a large bowl; stir in egg, lemon juice, dill, salt, and pepper.

3. Lay one sheet of phyllo dough on a clean work surface. Using a pastry brush, dab all over with melted butter; lay a second sheet on top. Cut the dough in half lengthwise.

4. Lay the two strips, with the narrow edges nearest you, on the work surface. Place ¼–⅓ cup spinach mixture at the bottom of each strip of dough. Top with 1 tablespoon feta.

5. Fold the dough flag style to form triangle-shaped packets: Fold the bottom-right corner to the left edge of the dough to form a triangle. Fold triangle along left edge of dough, then fold lower-left corner to the right edge of the dough. Seal any remaining top edge of dough to packet. The filling should be totally enclosed in the dough.

6. Wrap each pastry individually in plastic wrap. Divide evenly between the freezer bags.

7. Seal and freeze.

TO BAKE

1. Thaw pastries in the refrigerator or bake straight from the freezer.

2. Preheat the oven to 400°F.

3. Remove as many pastries as desired from the freezer. Remove plastic wrap. Place pastries on a greased baking sheet. Brush with melted butter. Bake 17 to 19 minutes if frozen, 14 to 16 minutes if thawed.

PHYLLO DOUGH

Phyllo can seem fussy but it's really quite forgiving. Though the sheets are paper-thin and can tear, the pastry is easily patched. Because this recipe calls for two sheets to be stacked and the final product is folded over and over, any damage to the dough is concealed.

This can be served to complement a meal as a side dish, or over rice as an entrée. —LT

THAI RED CURRY WITH VEGETABLES

MAKES 3 SIDE DISHES, 4 SERVINGS EACH, OR 2 ENTRÉES, 4 SERVINGS EACH

2 (15-ounce) cans coconut milk

½ cup chicken broth

2 tablespoons fish sauce

2 teaspoons red curry paste

1 teaspoon honey

½ pound fresh white mushrooms, cleaned and sliced

1 cup sliced carrots (about 2 medium)

1 (15-ounce) can baby corn, drained

1 (8-ounce) can bamboo shoots, drained

2 or 3 one-gallon freezer bags, labeled

1. Combine coconut milk, broth, fish sauce, curry paste, and honey in a medium saucepan; heat gently over medium heat. Add mushrooms; cook, stirring, for 5 minutes. Add carrots; cook, stirring, 5 minutes longer. Cool.

2. Divide cooled vegetable mixture evenly among the freezer bags. (Use 3 bags for side dish portions; 2 bags for entrée portions.) Divide corn and bamboo shoots evenly over vegetables.

3. Seal and freeze.

TO COOK ONE SIDE DISH OR ENTRÉE

1. Completely thaw one bag in the refrigerator.

2. Pour sauce and vegetables into a medium saucepan; warm over medium heat. Serve as a side dish or as an entrée over steamed rice.

HEAT WARNING

This dish is on the spicy side. The red curry paste supplies all the heat, so adjust that ingredient if you want less fire.

Many families find their holiday dinner table shared by vegetarians and meat eaters alike. This dish makes a satisfying vegetarian entrée accompanied by a variety of sides, or it makes a wonderful side dish to your turkey or ham. —KN

WILD RICE AND NUT BAKE

MAKES 4 ENTRÉES, 6 SERVINGS EACH

8½ CUPS COOKED WILD RICE BLEND, COOLED (ABOUT 2¾–3 CUPS UNCOOKED RICE BLEND)

10 cups Cheddar-Jack cheese blend (about 2½ pounds total, or 1¼ pounds of each)

6 cups milk

12 eggs, lightly beaten

4 cups diced onion (about 4 medium)

2 cups pine nuts (about 5 ounces)

1½ cups chopped pecans (about 6 ounces)

1½ cups chopped walnuts (6 ounces)

¼ cup dried parsley

4 one-gallon freezer bags, labeled

1. Mix rice, cheeses, milk, eggs, onions, pine nuts, pecans, walnuts, and parsley in a large bowl. The mixture will be wet.

2. Divide evenly among the freezer bags.

3. Seal and freeze.

TO COOK ONE ENTRÉE

1. Completely thaw one entrée in the refrigerator.

2. Preheat the oven to 350°F.

3. Put the rice and nut mixture in a greased baking dish. Bake, uncovered, for 1 to 1½ hours, or until set and a knife inserted into the center comes out clean.

EXTRA SUPPORT

It can be difficult to fill freezer bags if they don't have enough support — not to mention the mess floppy bags can cause. To make the bags easy to fill, place them in cracker boxes, cottage cheese tubs, or other rigid containers. Fold the top of the bag over the container rim before filling. For other helpful packaging tips, see page 15.

Substitute scallops for the shrimp in this dish to create an equally tasty entrée. Serve over rice with any of the following toppings: toasted shredded coconut, toasted sliced almonds, apple pieces, pineapple tidbits, raisins, dried cranberries, chopped scallions, mango chutney, hot chili paste, or sweet chili sauce. —LT

SHRIMP CURRY

MAKES 3 ENTRÉES, 4–6 SERVINGS EACH

2 POUNDS CLEANED AND COOKED PRAWNS OR SHRIMP, FRESH OR FROZEN

1 cup (2 sticks) butter

2 cups chopped onion (about 2 medium)

¼ cup curry powder

2 tablespoons minced ginger

2 tablespoons minced garlic (about 18 cloves)

2 tablespoons sugar

2 tablespoons chicken bouillon granules

1 tablespoon salt

1½ cups all-purpose flour

4 cups water

4 cups milk

2 tablespoons lemon juice

3–9 one-gallon freezer bags, label 3

1. Melt butter in a large saucepan over medium heat. Add onions and cook, stirring, until soft, about 5 minutes. Add curry, ginger, garlic, sugar, bouillon, and salt; cook, stirring, for 2 minutes. Add flour; cook, stirring, 2 minutes longer. Mixture will be like a paste.

2. Gradually add water and milk; cook, stirring constantly, until the sauce has thickened. Add lemon juice only after sauce has thickened. Cool sauce.

IF USING FRESH, COOKED SHRIMP

1. Divide shrimp evenly among the three labeled freezer bags. Divide cooled sauce evenly over shrimp.

2. Seal and freeze.

IF USING FROZEN, COOKED SHRIMP

1. Divide shrimp evenly among three of the unlabeled 1-gallon bags. Divide the cooled sauce evenly among three other unlabeled bags. Seal bags. Into each labeled bag, place a bag of shrimp and a bag of sauce.

2. Seal and freeze.

TO COOK ONE ENTRÉE

1. Completely thaw one entrée in the refrigerator.

2. In a large skillet over medium heat, bring the shrimp and curry sauce to a simmer. Do not boil. Serve over rice.

Once I discovered how much easier it is to make lasagna by using uncooked noodles, I decided to revisit manicotti; I had long ago given up on struggling with the limp, easily torn cooked manicotti noodles. This entrée is a favorite that I like to give to a friend or neighbor in need of a meal. —LT

MANICOTTI

MAKES 4 ENTRÉES, 4 SERVINGS EACH

1 (48-OUNCE) CONTAINER COTTAGE CHEESE (6 CUPS)

2 eggs, lightly beaten

3 cups shredded mozzarella cheese (about 12 ounces)

1 cup shredded Parmesan cheese

½ teaspoon salt

½ teaspoon black pepper

2 (8-ounce) boxes manicotti (12–14 shells in each box), uncooked

12 cups Basic Red Sauce (page178)

Four 8-inch square baking dishes

Plastic wrap

Aluminum foil

1. Mix cottage cheese, eggs, mozzarella, Parmesan, salt, and pepper in a large bowl. With your fingers or a spoon, stuff filling into manicotti shells.

2. Spread ½ cup of red sauce in the bottom of each baking dish. Place six or seven manicotti in each dish. Divide remaining red sauce evenly over the four dishes of manicotti. Wrap each dish entirely in plastic wrap.

3. Top with foil, label, and freeze.

TO COOK ONE ENTRÉE

1. Thaw one entrée in the refrigerator or bake it straight from the freezer.

2. Preheat the oven to 350°F.

3. Remove plastic wrap and foil from baking dish and replace foil. Bake for 45 minutes if thawed, 1 hour if frozen. Remove foil and continue baking until the noodles are tender.

For years I made only vegetarian lasagna. Meat seemed unnecessary because the vegetables were so tasty. This recipe uses less red sauce than the classic version because the vegetables themselves add moisture. —LT

VEGETABLE LASAGNA: LARGE PAN

MAKES 2 ENTRÉES, 12 SERVINGS EACH

1 (48-OUNCE) CONTAINER COTTAGE CHEESE (6 CUPS)

4 eggs, lightly beaten

3 cups shredded Parmesan cheese, divided into 2 cups and 1 cup

11 cups Basic Red Sauce (page 178)

18 lasagna noodles, uncooked

4 cups assorted vegetables in bite-size pieces (mushrooms, zucchini, carrots, onions, green and red bell peppers are nice)

8 cups shredded mozzarella cheese (about 2 pounds)

Two 13- by 9- by 2-inch baking dishes

Plastic wrap

Aluminum foil

1. Mix cottage cheese, eggs, and 2 cups of the Parmesan in a large bowl.

2. Lay baking dishes before you and spread ½ cup red sauce in the bottom of each.

3. Assemble both lasagnas at once in layers in the following order:

   LAYER 1
   3 uncooked noodles
   1½ cups red sauce
   1 cup vegetables
   1½ cups cottage cheese mixture
   1 cup mozzarella

   LAYER 2
   3 uncooked noodles
   1½ cups red sauce
   1 cup vegetables – or whatever remains

   1½ cups cottage cheese mixture – or whatever remains
   1 cup mozzarella

   LAYER 3
   3 uncooked noodles
   2 cups red sauce – or whatever remains
   2 cups mozzarella
   ½ cup Parmesan

4. Wrap each dish entirely in plastic wrap. Top with foil, label, and freeze.

TO COOK ONE ENTRÉE

1. Thaw one entrée in the refrigerator or bake it straight from the freezer.

2. Preheat the oven to 375°F.

3. Remove plastic wrap and foil from baking dish and replace foil. Place dish on a rimmed baking sheet and bake for 1 hour if thawed, 1½ hours if frozen. Remove foil and continue baking until lasagna is bubbling and cheese is browned.

These smaller lasagnas are the perfect size for giving away. —LT

VEGETABLE LASAGNA: SMALL PAN

MAKES 4 ENTRÉES, 4–6 SERVINGS EACH

1 (48-OUNCE) CONTAINER COTTAGE CHEESE (6 CUPS)

4 eggs, lightly beaten

3 cups shredded Parmesan cheese, divided into 2 cups and 1 cup

11 cups Basic Red Sauce (page 178)

24 lasagna noodles, uncooked

4 cups assorted vegetables in bite-size pieces (mushrooms, zucchini, carrots, onions, green and red bell peppers are nice)

8 cups shredded mozzarella cheese (about 2 pounds)

Four 12½- by 6½- by 3-inch foil loaf pans

Plastic wrap

Aluminum foil

1. Mix cottage cheese, eggs, and 2 cups of the Parmesan in a large bowl.

2. Lay baking dishes before you and spread ¼ cup red sauce in the bottom of each.

3. Assemble all four lasagnas at once in layers in the following order:

   LAYER 1
   2 uncooked noodles
   ¾ cup red sauce
   ½ cup vegetables
   ¾ cup cottage cheese mixture
   ½ cup mozzarella

   LAYER 2
   2 uncooked noodles
   ¾ cup red sauce
   ½ cup vegetables – or whatever remains

   ¾ cup cottage cheese mixture – or whatever remains
   ½ cup mozzarella

   LAYER 3
   2 uncooked noodles
   1 cup red sauce – or whatever remains
   1 cup mozzarella
   ¼ cup Parmesan

4. Wrap each pan entirely in plastic wrap. Top with foil, label, and freeze.

TO COOK ONE ENTRÉE

1. Thaw one entrée in the refrigerator or bake it straight from the freezer.

2. Preheat the oven to 375°F.

3. Remove plastic wrap and foil from baking dish and replace foil. Bake for 45 minutes if thawed, 1 hour if frozen. Remove foil and continue baking until lasagna is bubbling and cheese is browned.

Perfect with pork or chicken dishes, I have even been known to serve it for dessert. —LT

APPLES AND CHEDDAR

MAKES 3 SIDE DISHES, 8 SERVINGS EACH

5 POUNDS TART APPLES, PEELED, CORED, AND SLICED

1 pound sharp Cheddar cheese, shredded

3 cups half-and-half (or light cream)

1½ teaspoons salt

TOPPING

3 cups (12 ounces) pecan halves

6 tablespoons brown sugar

3 teaspoons butter

6 *one-gallon freezer bags, label 3*

3 sandwich bags

ON HAND FOR COOKING EACH SIDE DISH

Aluminum foil

1. Divide apples and cheese among the three unlabeled 1-gallon freezer bags. Into each bag, measure 1 cup half-and-half and ½ teaspoon salt. Seal bags.

2. Into each sandwich bag, measure 1 cup pecan halves, 2 tablespoons brown sugar, and 1 teaspoon butter. Seal bags.

3. Into each labeled 1-gallon freezer bag, place one bag apple mixture and one bag pecan mixture.

4. Seal and freeze.

TO COOK ONE SIDE DISH

1. Completely thaw one side dish in the refrigerator.

2. Preheat the oven to 350°F.

3. Put apple mixture in an ungreased baking dish and cover tightly with foil. Bake for 45 minutes. Remove foil and continue baking until apples are soft and sauce is reduced and bubbly.

4. Meanwhile, put pecan mixture in a small skillet and add 1 tablespoon water. Cook, stirring, over medium heat for 5 minutes, or until pecans and sauce caramelize. Remove from heat. Cool and crumble over baked apples.

This soup is a treat! Make this when fresh asparagus is abundant. —LT

CREAM OF ASPARAGUS SOUP

MAKES ABOUT 8 CUPS

2 POUNDS FRESH ASPARAGUS, CLEANED AND FIBROUS ENDS SNAPPED OFF

4 cups chicken broth

¼ cup chopped onion

1 large carrot, cut into 2-inch pieces

1 cup heavy cream

1 teaspoon salt

1 teaspoon black pepper

2 one-quart freezer bags or 1 one-gallon freezer bag, labeled

1. Place asparagus in a large shallow pan with just enough water to cover. Bring to a boil. Reduce heat and simmer for 4 minutes. Drain water, reserving 1 cup. Cut asparagus into 2-inch pieces and set aside.

2. Return reserved water to pan. Add broth, onion, and carrot and simmer until vegetables are soft, about 10 minutes.

3. Put broth, vegetables, and asparagus in a blender; blend until smooth (some small chunks of asparagus are okay). Stir in cream, salt, and pepper. Cool.

4. Divide cooled soup evenly between two 1-quart bags, or pour into 1-gallon bag.

5. Seal and freeze.

TO ENJOY

1. Completely thaw one bag in the refrigerator.

2. Reheat soup in a medium saucepan over low heat.

MORE SOUP?

Using the warehouse size asparagus in this recipe means the yield is smaller than that of our other recipes. Feel free to multiply the recipe, but take care with the seasonings — see our advice about adapting recipes on page 212.

Not only is it convenient to have a main dish prepared ahead of time, but it can be equally satisfying to serve a side dish with no extra fuss at dinner time. —LT

GARLIC MASHED POTATOES

MAKES 4 SIDE DISHES, 6 SERVINGS EACH

10 POUNDS RUSSET POTA-TOES, PEELED AND CUT INTO LARGE CHUNKS

1 tablespoon olive oil

2 tablespoons minced garlic

2 (8-ounce) packages cream cheese, cut into quarters

1 teaspoon salt

1 teaspoon black pepper

1 cup chicken broth

Four 8-inch square baking dishes

Plastic wrap

Aluminum foil

1. Put potatoes in a large stockpot with water to cover. Bring to a boil and cook potatoes until they break apart easily with a fork, 9 to 12 minutes.

2. Meanwhile, heat oil in a small skillet over medium heat. Add garlic and cook, stirring occasionally, until soft, about 3 minutes. Remove pan from heat.

3. Drain potatoes and return them to the pot. Add garlic with oil, cream cheese, salt, and pepper; mash potatoes. Stir in chicken broth. Divide potatoes evenly among the baking dishes. Wrap each dish entirely in plastic wrap and cover with foil.

4. Label and freeze.

TO COOK ONE SIDE DISH

1. Thaw one side dish in the refrigerator or bake straight from the freezer.

2. Preheat the oven to 350°F.

3. Remove plastic wrap and foil from baking dish and replace foil. Bake for 1 hour if frozen, 30 minutes if thawed, or until potatoes are hot all the way through.

This hearty soup is filling enough for dinner but makes a great quick lunch, too. —LT

BAKED POTATO CHOWDER

MAKES 4 ENTRÉES, 6 SERVINGS EACH

10 POUNDS RUSSET POTA-TOES, BAKED AND COOLED

1 cup (2 sticks) butter

2 cups chopped onion (about 2 medium)

¼ cup dried parsley

2 tablespoons beef bouillon granules

1 tablespoon minced garlic (about 9 cloves)

1 tablespoon dried basil

2 teaspoons salt

2 teaspoons black pepper

2 cups all-purpose flour

12 cups water

4 cups half-and-half (or light cream)

1 pound sharp Cheddar cheese, cut into large chunks

4 one-gallon freezer bags, labeled

1. Cut potatoes in half; scoop out flesh. Set potato aside and discard skins, or save for another use (see Note below).

2. Melt butter in a large stockpot over medium heat. Add onions and cook, stirring, until soft, about 5 minutes. Add parsley, bouillon, garlic, basil, salt, and pepper; cook, stirring, for 2 minutes. Add flour; cook, stirring, 2 minutes longer. Mixture will be like a paste. Gradually add water, half-and-half, and potato; cook, stirring frequently, until soup has thickened, about 30 minutes. Add cheese; cook, stirring, until melted. Cool.

3. Divide cooled soup evenly among the freezer bags. Seal and freeze.

TO COOK ONE ENTRÉE

1. Completely thaw one entrée in the refrigerator.

2. Bring the soup to a simmer in a large saucepan over medium heat. Do not boil.

SAVE THOSE SKINS!

Potato skins make a fun snack. Sprinkle with dried or fresh herbs, crumbled bacon, and shredded cheese. Broil in the oven until cheese melts. Serve with sour cream or guacamole. Or, just spread them with a bit of butter and sprinkle with salt and pepper. Yum!

This is a delicious and easy-to-make variation on our Classic Chili (page 94). When I know I'll be feeding a mixed crowd of vegetarians and meat eaters, I simply give guests a choice between the two. —LT

BLACK BEAN AND VEGETABLE CHILI

MAKES 4 ENTRÉES, 8 SERVINGS EACH

1 POUND FRESH WHITE MUSHROOMS, CLEANED AND SLICED

6 cups sliced carrots
(about 12 medium carrots)

6 cups sliced celery
(about 12 stalks)

4 cups chopped onion
(about 4 medium)

2 large green bell peppers, cut into 1-inch pieces

12 cups Basic Red Sauce
(page 178)

8 (15-ounce) cans kidney beans

4 (15-ounce) cans black beans

4 tablespoons chili powder

4 tablespoons hot pepper sauce

4 teaspoons minced garlic

4 teaspoons dried oregano

4 teaspoons black pepper

4 one-gallon freezer bags, labeled

1. Into each freezer bag measure one-quarter of the mushrooms, 1½ cups carrots, 1½ cups celery, 1 cup onions, one-quarter of the bell peppers, 3 cups red sauce, 2 cans kidney beans, 1 can black beans, 1 tablespoon chili powder, 1 tablespoon hot pepper sauce, 1 teaspoon garlic, 1 teaspoon oregano, and 1 teaspoon black pepper.

2. Seal and freeze.

TO COOK ONE ENTRÉE

1. Completely thaw one entrée in the refrigerator.

2. Cook chili in a medium saucepan over medium-low heat for 1 hour, or until liquid cooks off and chili is thick.

I took an old family recipe and enlivened it. You'll love this simple supper. —LT

SEAFOOD CREOLE

MAKES 3 ENTRÉES, 6–8 SERVINGS EACH

3 (46-ounce) cans/bottles vegetable juice (such as V8)

3 large green bell peppers, diced

3 large onions, diced

3 large celery stalks, diced

3 tablespoons minced garlic (about 27 cloves)

3 teaspoons paprika

3 teaspoons salt

3 teaspoons black pepper

3 teaspoons dried parsley

¾ teaspoon celery seed

¾ teaspoon cayenne pepper

4½ pounds bite-size pieces of seafood in any combination (shrimp, scallops, crabmeat, halibut, cod)

6 one-gallon freezer bags, label 3

3 one-quart bags

1. Using a large, sturdy container to hold the bag (see also page 15 for method), carefully pour one container of vegetable juice into each unlabeled 1-gallon bag. Divide the bell peppers, onions, and celery evenly among the bags of juice. Into each bag measure 1 tablespoon garlic, 1 teaspoon paprika, 1 teaspoon salt, 1 teaspoon black pepper, 1 teaspoon parsley, ¼ teaspoon celery seed, and ¼ teaspoon cayenne. Seal bags.

2. Into each 1-quart bag, measure 1½ pounds seafood. Place a bag of vegetable juice mixture and a bag of seafood into each labeled 1-gallon bag.

3. Seal and freeze.

TO COOK ONE ENTRÉE

1. Completely thaw one entrée in the refrigerator.

2. Bring vegetable juice mixture to a boil in a large saucepan. Reduce heat and simmer for 20 minutes. Add seafood and continue simmering until seafood is thoroughly cooked, 5 to 7 minutes. Serve over rice.

This soup is ideal for lunch. Forget canned and condensed — make the real thing for yourself and taste the difference. —LT

CREAM OF MUSHROOM SOUP

MAKES ABOUT 10 CUPS

2½ POUNDS FRESH WHITE MUSHROOMS, CLEANED AND SLICED

½ cup (1 stick) butter

½ cup all-purpose flour

4 cups chicken broth

1 teaspoon salt

1 teaspoon black pepper

2 cups heavy cream

3 one-quart or 2 one-gallon freezer bags, labeled

1. Melt butter in a large stockpot over medium heat. Add mushrooms and cook, stirring, until soft, about 10 minutes. Add flour; cook, stirring, for 2 minutes longer. Add broth, salt, and pepper; cook, stirring, until soup is smooth and has thickened, about 5 minutes longer. Stir in cream. Cool.

2. Divide cooled soup evenly among the freezer bags.

3. Seal and freeze

TO ENJOY

1. Completely thaw one bag in the refrigerator.

2. Reheat soup in a medium saucepan over low heat.

CHICKEN BROTH IN A VEGETABLE SOUP?

We love the flavor of chicken broth, but you can make this or any of our other meatless soups vegetarian by substituting vegetable broth for the chicken or beef broth.

The amount of Roma tomatoes called for in this recipe matches the package sizes offered in warehouse clubs. The flavor of this tomato soup is unique, I found, and I wanted to be sure to share it with our readers. We've made only minor changes to Carol Costenbader's original recipe in *The Big Book of Preserving the Harvest*. —KN

TOMATO-BASIL SOUP

MAKES 3 ENTRÉES, 4 SERVINGS EACH

½ cup (1 stick) butter

3 cups chopped onion
(about 3 medium)

1 teaspoon minced garlic
(about 3 cloves)

3 pounds Roma tomatoes, chopped

8 cups chicken broth

1 tablespoon lime juice

Pinch of sugar

¾ cup chopped fresh basil leaves

Zest of one orange

3 one-gallon freezer bags, labeled

1. Melt butter in a stockpot over low heat. Add onions and cook, stirring, until soft, about 15 minutes. Add garlic; cook, stirring, 2 minutes. Add tomatoes, broth, lime juice, and sugar; bring to a boil. Reduce heat and simmer, covered, for 15 minutes. Stir in basil and orange zest.

2. Let soup cool slightly; transfer to a food processor and purée. Cool completely. Divide cooled soup evenly among the freezer bags.

3. Seal and freeze.

TO COOK ONE ENTRÉE

1. Completely thaw one entrée in the refrigerator.

2. Reheat soup in a medium saucepan over medium-low heat.

RESOURCES

Carol's book has several other recipes that use warehouse-size packaging. Try her Barbecued Beef Jerky and Lemon-Pineapple Preserves, for example. Carol also devotes a chapter to home-freezing techniques, with in-depth discussion of how to prepare fresh fruits, vegetables, and herbs for the freezer. Her book, like many listed in the resources section (page 241), is a good companion to ours.

If you're an onion lover, this soup is for you. I like to freeze this in complete packages: soup, bread, and cheese. That way, I don't need to have anything particular on hand when I want to serve it. —LT

FRENCH ONION SOUP

MAKES 5 ENTRÉES, 4 SERVINGS EACH

10 POUNDS ONIONS, PEELED AND CUT IN HALF

½ cup olive oil

½ cup (1 stick) butter

1 tablespoon salt

2 tablespoons beef bouillon granules

2 tablespoons Worcestershire sauce

1 tablespoon minced garlic (about 9 cloves)

1 tablespoon black pepper

5 cups shredded Swiss or Gouda cheese (about 1¼ pounds)

20 small slices French bread, toasted

10 one-gallon freezer bags, label 5

5 sandwich bags

ON HAND FOR COOKING EACH ENTRÉE

4 cups boiling water

1. Place onion halves cut side down and slice into ½-inch strips.

2. Heat oil and butter in a large stockpot over medium heat. Add onions and salt. Cook, stirring frequently, for 1 hour. Reduce heat if onions begin to brown. Add bouillon, Worcestershire sauce, garlic, and pepper; cook, stirring, 10 minutes longer. Cool.

3. Divide cooled onion mixture among the unlabeled 1-gallon freezer bags. Seal bags.

4. Into each of the sandwich bags, measure 1 cup cheese. Seal bags.

5. Into each of the five labeled 1-gallon freezer bags, place one bag of onion mixture, one bag of cheese, and 4 slices of French bread.

6. Seal and freeze.

TO COOK ONE ENTRÉE

1. Completely thaw one entrée in the refrigerator.

2. Preheat the oven broiler.

3. Place four ovenproof bowls on a rimmed baking sheet and divide onion mixture among them. Add 1 cup boiling water to each bowl. Top each soup with a slice of French bread. Divide the cheese evenly over the bread slices. Broil just until cheese melts and browns. Take care when serving the soup: the bowls will be very hot.

CHAPTER FIVE

SAUCES, MARINADES, AND FLAVORED BUTTERS

One spring a couple years ago I thought it would be a good idea to order 10 sauce-tomato starts for the garden. The plants must have thought it was a good idea, too, since they rewarded me with hundreds of delicious tomatoes at the end of summer. Tomatoes from the warehouse work perfectly in this recipe also, as they're sold in 2- to 3-pound packages. If you don't grow your own, buy them at the club. —KN

CHIPOTLE ROASTED-TOMATO SAUCE

MAKES 7–10 CUPS

7½–9 POUNDS FRESH ROMA TOMATOES

6 chipotle peppers canned in adobo sauce, halved and seeded

1½ pounds onions, sliced

1½ teaspoons vegetable oil

½ teaspoon salt (optional)

7 one-pint freezer bags, labeled

1. Preheat the oven to 475°F.

2. Rinse and slice tomatoes in half lengthwise. Arrange in a single layer in several baking dishes. Sprinkle salt over the tomatoes. Add chipotle peppers and onions to each baking dish; mix to combine. Drizzle oil over the vegetable mixture. Bake for 30 to 35 minutes, or until tomatoes are soft and onions are beginning to brown.

3. Cool tomatoes enough to handle. Slide skins off. Remove chipotle peppers and discard.

4. Using a food processor and working in batches, spoon tomatoes and onions into processor's bowl with a slotted spoon so that the juices can drain back into dish. Purée tomatoes and onions until smooth. Add juices from the baking dish if sauce is too thick. Discard remaining juice.

5. Divide sauce among freezer bags.

6. Seal and freeze.

TO ENJOY

1. Completely thaw one bag in the refrigerator.

2. Use in a recipe calling for tomato sauce for a chipotle-enlivened dish, or simmer in a medium saucepan over medium-low heat for 5 to 10 minutes and pour over your favorite pasta.

RECIPE SUGGESTIONS

Our Chipotle Roasted-Tomato Sauce is excellent with cheese ravioli and other pasta dishes. You will also find it in: Cinco Layer Bake (page 62) and the Tex-Mex variation of Cajun Braised Skillet Chops (page 116).

We use the Basic Red Sauce on the following page in many more recipes. It's a true staple in our freezers. You will find it in: Beef Barley Soup (page 104), Black Bean and Vegetable Chili (page 168), Chicken Parmigiana (page 28), Classic Chili (page 94), Classic Lasagna (page 80), Feta and Spinach Lasagna Rolls (page 152), Manicotti (page 159), Pork Loin Ragout (page 133), Pork Ragout Lasagna (page 134), Spanish Rice (page 85), Vegetable Lasagna (page 160).

This all-purpose tomato sauce is used in some of the recipes in this book. It can be used anywhere a red sauce is needed. This simple sauce is not cooked before it's frozen. Six to eight cups is a good amount to package for a meal for four to six people. —LT

BASIC RED SAUCE: LARGE BATCH

MAKES ABOUT 40 CUPS, OR 10 QUARTS, OR 2½ GALLONS

1 (111-OUNCE) CAN TOMATO PASTE, HALVED (SEE NOTE), OR 4 (12-OUNCE) CANS

8 cups hot water

½ cup dried parsley

½ cup minced onion

¼ cup minced garlic (about 36 cloves)

¼ cup sugar

2 tablespoons salt

2 teaspoons dried basil

2 teaspoons dried oregano

2 teaspoons dried thyme

1 (106-ounce) can tomato sauce, or 4 (28-ounce) cans

1 (102-ounce) can diced tomatoes, or 4 (28-ounce) cans

Several 1-gallon freezer bags (number will vary)

NOTE: Use half of the tomato paste for this recipe and freeze the other half in a freezer container or freezer bag to use the next time you make this sauce.

1. Mix tomato paste and hot water in a large stockpot until smooth. Stir in parsley, onion, garlic, sugar, salt, basil, oregano, and thyme.

2. Add tomato sauce and diced tomatoes; mix well. Do not cook.

3. Measure sauce into appropriate portions for immediate use. Divide remaining sauce evenly among 1-gallon freezer bags for later use.

4. Seal and label each bag with the amount of sauce inside. Freeze.

TO ENJOY

1. Completely thaw one bag in the refrigerator.

2. Use in a recipe calling for tomato sauce, or simmer in a saucepan over medium-low heat for 20 minutes and pour over your favorite pasta.

3. To use in a meat sauce, brown and drain 1 pound lean ground beef for every 8 cups of sauce; add cooked beef to sauce and gently reheat.

BASIC RED SAUCE: SMALL BATCH

MAKES ABOUT 10 CUPS

1 (12-OUNCE) CAN TOMATO PASTE

2 cups hot water

2 tablespoons dried parsley

2 tablespoons minced onion

1 tablespoon minced garlic
(about 9 cloves)

1 tablespoon sugar

2 teaspoons salt

½ teaspoon dried basil

½ teaspoon dried oregano

½ teaspoon dried thyme

1 (28-ounce) can tomato sauce

1 (28-ounce) can diced tomatoes

*Several 1-quart freezer bags
(number will vary)*

1. Mix tomato paste and hot water in a large bowl until smooth. Stir in parsley, onion, garlic, sugar, salt, basil, oregano, and thyme.

2. Add tomato sauce and diced tomatoes; mix well. Do not cook.

3. Measure sauce into appropriate portions for immediate use. Divide remaining sauce evenly among 1-quart freezer bags for later use.

4. Seal and label each bag with the amount of sauce inside. Freeze.

TO ENJOY

1. Completely thaw one bag in the refrigerator.

2. Use in a recipe calling for tomato sauce, or simmer in a saucepan over medium-low heat for 20 minutes and pour over your favorite pasta.

3. To use in a meat sauce, brown and drain 1 pound lean ground beef for every 8 cups of sauce; add cooked beef to sauce and gently reheat.

"Yum!" says my four-year-old. —KN

BROWN SUGAR AND BOURBON
MARINADE FOR SALMON

MAKES 2 MARINADES, FOR 2 POUNDS SALMON EACH

2 cups orange juice

1 cup packed brown sugar

½ cup soy sauce

½ cup bourbon

4 tablespoons diced onion

2 teaspoons minced garlic
(about 6 cloves)

2 ounces (about a 2½-inch piece)
fresh ginger, peeled and cut into
1/8-inch-thick slices

*2 small square freezer containers,
labeled*

ON HAND FOR COOKING EACH ENTRÉE

2 POUNDS SALMON

1. Whisk together orange juice, brown sugar, soy sauce, and bourbon in a large bowl; divide evenly between the two freezer containers.

2. Into each container, measure 2 tablespoons onion and 1 teaspoon garlic. Divide the ginger slices evenly between the containers.

3. Seal and freeze.

TO USE THE MARINADE WITH FRESH FISH

1. Completely thaw one marinade in the refrigerator.

2. Place 2 pounds salmon in an ungreased 13- by 9-inch baking dish. Pour marinade over salmon and marinate 6 to 8 hours in the refrigerator.

3. Prepare a medium fire in a gas or charcoal grill.

4. Cook salmon, turning occasionally, for 10 to 15 minutes, or until fish flakes easily with a fork. Discard remaining marinade.

This compound butter offers a great way to use up pecans left over from holiday baking. I wrote this recipe to yield an ample amount for those large holiday gatherings of friends and family. Toss with green beans or roasted red potatoes. —KN

GORGONZOLA-PECAN BUTTER

MAKES 4 BUTTER LOGS, ABOUT 1/3 CUP EACH

1 cup unsalted butter, softened

⅔ cup finely crumbled Gorgonzola cheese

2 tablespoons pecans, finely chopped

Wax paper

1 one-quart freezer bag, labeled

1. Mix butter, Gorgonzola, and pecans in a medium bowl.

2. Divide mixture in quarters and place each portion on a sheet of wax paper. Roll paper tightly so that the butter takes the shape of a log; place all four butter logs in the freezer bag.

3. Seal and freeze.

TO ENJOY

Completely thaw one butter log in the refrigerator. Store in an airtight container in the refrigerator for up to 2 weeks or in the freezer for up to 1 month.

Compound butters spruce up a plain seafood dish, a baked potato, or pasta. We enjoy this one on salmon straight from the grill. —KN

WALNUT-PESTO BUTTER

MAKES 2 LOGS, FOR 2 POUNDS SALMON EACH

1 cup (2 sticks) butter, softened

⅓ cup pesto (try our handmade version on page 185)

2 tablespoons finely chopped walnuts

Wax paper

1 one-quart freezer bag, labeled

ON HAND FOR COOKING EACH ENTRÉE

2 POUNDS SALMON

1. Blend butter and pesto in a small bowl with a wooden spoon or scraper. Stir in walnuts.

2. Divide mixture in half and place each portion on a sheet of wax paper. Roll paper tightly so that the butter takes the shape of a log; place both butter logs in the freezer bag. Seal and freeze.

TO USE THE MARINADE WITH FRESH FISH

1. Completely thaw one butter log in the refrigerator.

2. Prepare a medium fire in a gas or charcoal grill.

3. Cook salmon, turning occasionally, for 10 to 15 minutes, or until fish flakes easily with a fork. Top salmon with butter.

FREEZING DETAILS

Compound butters can be stored in the freezer for up to 1 month and in the refrigerator for 2 weeks.

Having a main dish finished and in the freezer is like having a basic black dress in the closet. And just as the accessories complete the outfit, having the main dish out of the way means that I can explore new ways to accessorize my meal. Compound butters like this one can be enjoyed tossed with steamed or roasted vegetables or pasta. —KN

GORGONZOLA LEMON-PEPPER BUTTER

MAKES 2 BUTTER LOGS, ABOUT 1/3 CUP EACH

½ cup unsalted butter, softened

1 tablespoon lemon pepper seasoning salt

⅓ cup finely crumbled Gorgonzola cheese

Wax paper

1 one-quart freezer bag, labeled

1. Blend butter and lemon pepper salt in a small bowl. Stir in Gorgonzola.

2. Divide mixture in half and place each portion on a sheet of wax paper.

3. Roll paper tightly so that the butter takes the shape of a log; place both butter logs in the freezer bag.

4. Seal and freeze.

TO ENJOY

Completely thaw one butter log in the refrigerator. Store in an airtight container in the refrigerator for up to 2 weeks or in the freezer for up to 1 month.

SALT-FREE VARIATION

For those interested in eliminating the salt but not the flavor of this butter, in place of the seasoning salt try a salt-free seasoning, such as Penzeys Florida Seasoned Pepper. (See resources, page 241.)

Halibut is my favorite fish. A cold-water fish, it has firm flesh and a mild flavor. If you can't find halibut, substitute another white fish such as cod or tilapia. —LT

CHILI-LIME BUTTER FOR HALIBUT

MAKES 2 COMPOUND BUTTERS, FOR 2 POUNDS HALIBUT EACH

¼ cup (½ stick) butter, softened

¼ cup olive oil

2 tablespoons soy sauce

2 tablespoons lime juice

2 teaspoons minced garlic

2 teaspoons dried oregano

2 teaspoons chili powder

½ teaspoon ground cumin

2 small square freezer containers, labeled

ON HAND FOR COOKING EACH ENTRÉE

2 pounds halibut

1. Combine butter, olive oil, soy sauce, lime juice, garlic, oregano, chili powder, and cumin in a small bowl. Divide mixture evenly between the two freezer containers.

2. Seal and freeze.

TO USE THE BUTTER WITH FRESH FISH

1. Completely thaw one container of butter in the refrigerator. Grease a baking dish with some of the Chili-Lime Butter.

2. Preheat the oven to 400°F.

3. Place the fish in the baking dish. Cover with the remaining butter compound and bake, uncovered, for 20 minutes, or until fish is opaque and flakes easily with a fork.

LEFTOVER FISH?

Any leftover baked fish is perfect in fish tacos! Fill warm corn tortillas with Chili-Lime Halibut, shredded Napa cabbage, and fresh cilantro. Add a squeeze of fresh lime, a drizzle of salsa, and a dollop of sour cream.

DO AHEAD

If you prefer, you can freeze the halibut with the compound butter: Into each of two labeled 1-gallon freezer bags, place 2 pounds of halibut. Divide the butter between the bags. Seal and freeze. Bake as directed above.

Pesto is such a simple sauce to make that you'll wonder why you ever purchased it. An additional benefit of doing it yourself is that you can alter ingredients to suit your preferences — make it more garlicky, cheesy, or nutty. Make a lot of it in summer when fresh basil is abundant. Pesto freezes beautifully. —LT

PERFECT PESTO

MAKES 1 ⅓ CUPS

2 cups packed fresh basil leaves

¾ cup shredded Parmesan cheese

¾ cup olive oil

½ cup walnuts or sunflower seeds

1½ teaspoons minced garlic
(about 5 cloves)

1. Combine all ingredients in a food processor or blender and blend until smooth.

2. Use immediately, or store, with a thin layer of olive oil on top, in an airtight container in the refrigerator for up to three days or in the freezer for up to 3 months.

VERSATILE NUTS

Although customarily pine nuts are used in pesto, I find walnuts or sunflower seeds more convenient and I prefer their taste, too. Substitute pine nuts if you prefer a more traditional flavor.

This recipe was developed for those who would rather not use a commercially prepared product for the Berry-Roasted Chicken (page 60). You can use this vinaigrette any way you like, of course. I like it over a salad of robust greens such as arugula and dandelion, or subtle greens such as romaine and butter lettuce, garnished with crumbled blue cheese and toasted pecans. —LT

RASPBERRY VINAIGRETTE

MAKES 1¾ CUPS

1 CUP OLIVE OIL

½ cup fresh or frozen raspberries, at room temperature

½ cup red wine vinegar

1 tablespoon balsamic vinegar

1 tablespoon honey

1 teaspoon spicy brown mustard

½ teaspoon salt

¼ teaspoon black pepper

1. Place all ingredients in a container with a tight-fitting lid. Shake vigorously.

2. Use immediately, or store in an airtight container in the refrigerator for up to 1 week. Bring to room temperature before serving.

BERRY-ROASTED CHICKEN

Even though this recipe doesn't yield quite the 2 cups called for in our Berry-Roasted Chicken recipe, simply divide the amount here between the two chickens — it'll work just as well.

This simple teriyaki sauce is just as tasty and convenient as anything you might buy in the store — but less expensive. Use it in our Teriyaki Chicken (page 59), or in other recipes, like the Rose City Teriyaki (page 97). —LT

TERIYAKI SAUCE

MAKES 2 CUPS

1 cup soy sauce

1 cup packed brown sugar

¼ cup red wine vinegar

1 tablespoon vegetable oil

2 teaspoons minced garlic

2 teaspoons minced ginger

1. Whisk together soy sauce, brown sugar, vinegar, oil, garlic, and ginger in a small bowl. Mix until sugar is dissolved.

2. Use immediately, or store in an airtight container in the refrigerator for up to 1 week or in the freezer for up to 3 months.

BIG SAVINGS

Homemade teriyaki is easy to make and costs pennies on the dollar compared to the bottled, store-bought versions. Purchasing the ingredients at the warehouse club can compound your savings since soy sauce, red wine vinegar, and brown sugar can be 2 to 4 times more expensive at the grocery store.

CHAPTER SIX

BREAKFAST, SNACKS, AND SWEETS

My husband discovered breakfast burritos for sale one day at a local coffee stand. They have been the solution on more than one hectic morning when there was no time for a hot breakfast. The commercial ones were expensive, though, and we had no idea of their nutritional content, so I developed my own recipe. Now we often enjoy a hot, nutritious breakfast that needs no preparation in the morning. —LT

BREAKFAST BURRITOS

MAKES 20 BURRITOS

1 DOZEN EGGS, LIGHTLY BEATEN

3 pounds yellow-flesh potatoes, boiled and cut into bite-size pieces

1 cup sour cream

1 teaspoon salt

1 teaspoon black pepper

20 ten-inch flour tortillas

1 pound deli ham, cut into bite-size pieces

2 cups shredded Cheddar cheese (about 8 ounces)

Aluminum foil

4 one-gallon freezer bags, labeled

1. Scramble the eggs in a large greased skillet over medium heat until just set.

2. Combine potato, scrambled eggs, sour cream, salt, and pepper in a large bowl.

3. Lay all the tortillas out on a work surface. Divide the potato/egg mixture evenly among the tortillas (about ½ cup on each). Divide the ham and cheese evenly over the egg mixture.

4. Wrap each tortilla burrito-style, then wrap each individually in foil. Divide evenly among freezer bags. Seal and freeze.

TO COOK ONE ENTRÉE

Thaw the burritos in the refrigerator or reheat them straight from the freezer.

MICROWAVE

Remove foil, defrost, and reheat.

OVEN

Bake in foil at 375°F for 30 minutes if frozen, 300°F for 30 minutes if thawed.

SHREDDED CHEESE

It used to be that the customer paid a high price for the convenience of products such as shredded cheese. Not anymore, thanks to the warehouse clubs. Shredded Cheddar and mozzarella cheeses are readily available for about the same price per pound as the whole bricks, taking the economic factor out of the decision to use these products. The same does not hold true at the supermarket, however. The identical brand of shredded Cheddar cheese at the grocery store costs almost four times more per pound than at the warehouse. A 5-pound bag of shredded cheese is almost 20 cups, so if you have a lot left over, divide it among one-quart freezer bags and freeze for up to three months.

These biscuits have half the amount of butter of traditional biscuits, but you'd never know it by their rich flavor. Enjoy them with many of our entrées, especially the soups and chilis. —LT

CHEESE BISCUIT MIX

MAKES 8 BATCHES, 8 SERVINGS EACH

2 POUNDS SHARP CHEDDAR CHEESE, SHREDDED

16 cups all-purpose flour

⅔ cup baking powder

¼ cup sugar

1 tablespoon salt

2 cups (4 sticks) butter, cut into 1-inch cubes

8 one-gallon freezer bags, labeled

ON HAND FOR BAKING EACH BATCH

¾ cup milk

1. Combine cheese, flour, baking powder, sugar, and salt in a large bowl. Add butter; rub into flour until the butter is in tiny pieces. Divide the mixture evenly among the freezer bags.

2. Seal and freeze.

TO BAKE ONE BATCH

1. Completely thaw one batch in the refrigerator.

2. Preheat the oven to 425°F.

3. Put the mixture in a medium bowl. Add milk and stir to form a dough. Turn dough out onto a lightly floured work surface and knead until dough holds together. Pat into a circle 2 inches thick. Cut into 8 wedges.

4. Place wedges on an ungreased rimmed baking sheet. Bake for 15 to 20 minutes, or until biscuits are golden brown.

At my house, I pull these versatile snacks out of the freezer to serve spur-of-the-moment visitors, to give dinner guests something to snack on before the meal is ready, as a make-ahead appetizer for the busy holiday season, or as a warm snack for the family on a cold afternoon. You can vary these snacks by adding an olive or a nut to the center of each ball. —LT

CHEESE BITES

MAKES 8 DOZEN

2 POUNDS SHARP CHEDDAR CHEESE, SHREDDED

2 cups (4 sticks) butter, softened

5 cups all-purpose flour

1 teaspoon salt

½ teaspoon cayenne pepper

Small pimento-stuffed green olives, well drained (optional)

Raw pecan halves (optional)

8 one-quart freezer bags, labeled

1. Combine cheese, butter, flour, salt, and cayenne in a large bowl; knead into dough. Roll dough into 1-inch balls and place on an ungreased rimmed baking sheet.

2. If using olives, form each ball around 1 olive. If using pecans, press 1 pecan half onto each ball.

3. Place cheese balls in freezer for 30 minutes.

4. Remove cheese balls from freezer. Place a dozen into each freezer bag.

5. Seal and freeze.

TO BAKE ONE DOZEN CHEESE BITES

1. Thaw one bag in the refrigerator or bake straight from the freezer.

2. Preheat the oven to 425°F.

3. Place cheese balls 3 inches apart on an ungreased baking sheet. Do not flatten. Bake 15 to 17 minutes if frozen, 13 to 15 minutes if thawed.

My mom made granola from scratch when I was growing up, and to this day I cannot eat the boxed stuff from the store — it just doesn't compare! Here's my version of my mom's recipe. I keep this on hand, not just for my family to eat but also to give as birthday, housewarming, or hostess gifts. —LT

GRANOLA

MAKES 24 CUPS

12 CUPS OLD-FASHIONED ROLLED OATS

2 cups almonds, chopped

2 cups untoasted sesame seeds

2 cups raw hulled sunflower seeds

2 cups unsweetened shredded coconut

2 cups wheat germ

1 cup raisins

1 cup dried cranberries

1 cup whole wheat flour

1 tablespoon ground cinnamon

2 cups vegetable oil

2 cups honey

⅔ cup water

2 tablespoons vanilla extract

2 teaspoons salt

8 one-quart freezer bags, labeled

1. Mix oats, almonds, sesame seeds, sunflower seeds, coconut, wheat germ, raisins, cranberries, flour, and cinnamon in a large bowl.

2. Combine oil, honey, water, vanilla, and salt in a medium saucepan. Cook, stirring, over medium heat until sauce begins to boil. Remove from heat. Pour sauce over the oat mixture and mix well.

3. Divide granola evenly among the freezer bags.

4. Seal and freeze.

TO BAKE ONE PACKAGE

1. Preheat the oven to 275°F.

2. Place frozen granola on an ungreased baking sheet. Bake, stirring every 10 minutes, for 30 minutes, or until golden brown.

3. Cool and store in an airtight container.

NOT JUST FOR BREAKFAST

Although we most often eat granola in the morning with milk, it's also delicious eaten as a snack — sprinkle over yogurt or ice cream, or just eat by the handful!

My friend Renée, who has a relatively large family, created this recipe for those times when she needed something quick but nutritious for breakfast. I have modified her recipe, but I kept her main goal in mind: to create a breakfast cookie that was both nutritious and tasty. —LT

PB&J BREAKFAST COOKIES

MAKES ABOUT 32 COOKIES

1½ cups natural peanut butter

1 cup (2 sticks) butter

1 cup packed brown sugar

½ cup apricot jam, preferably no sugar added

¼ cup molasses

4 eggs

2 teaspoons vanilla extract

4 cups old-fashioned rolled oats

3 cups whole wheat flour

1 cup hulled sunflower seeds

1 cup instant dry milk powder

2 teaspoons baking soda

1 teaspoon salt

Wax paper

4 one-gallon freezer bags, labeled

1. Preheat the oven to 350°F.

2. Combine peanut butter, butter, brown sugar, jam, molasses, eggs, and vanilla in a food processor or by hand in a large bowl. Mix oats, flour, sunflower seeds, dry milk, baking soda, and salt in a separate large bowl. Pour the peanut butter mixture into the dry ingredients; mix well.

3. Scoop dough with a ¼-cup measure and place several inches apart on ungreased baking sheets. With your fingers or the back of a spoon, shape into 1-inch-thick patties. Bake for 13 to 16 minutes. Cool on baking sheets for 5 minutes; transfer to a cooling rack. Divide cooled cookies evenly among freezer bags, separating layers with wax paper.

4. Seal and freeze.

TO ENJOY

Remove desired number of cookies from freezer; thaw in the refrigerator or at room temperature.

BAKE BEFORE FREEZING?

Unlike our sweet-cookie recipes, we like to bake these before freezing so they're easy to grab in the morning. The dough does freeze well though, so if you prefer, freeze the dough as described in the cookie recipes beginning on page 203.

Like most children, my kids are nuts about the zoo. This snack mix has all the right stuff: peanuts for the little elephants, banana chips for the little monkeys, mango for the little bats, and berries for the birds. Each ingredient helps reinforce the wonder and fun of acting like our creature friends. Add to the fun by personalizing the snack bags to reflect the foods eaten by the animals at a zoo you frequent. Each snack bag holds enough for two children to share. —KN

ZOO DAY SNACK MIX

MAKES 6 SNACK BAGS

3 CUPS ANIMAL CRACKERS (6 OUNCES)

1½ cups banana chips (6 ounces)

12 tablespoons chopped dried mango (6 ounces)

12 tablespoons lightly salted peanuts (6 ounces)

12 tablespoons dried berries or raisins (6 ounces)

6 snack or sandwich bags

1 one-gallon freezer bag, labeled

1. Into each snack bag, place ½ cup animal crackers, ¼ cup banana chips, 2 tablespoons mangoes, 2 tablespoons peanuts, and 2 tablespoons berries. Seal bags and gently shake to combine ingredients; place snack bags in the 1-gallon freezer bag.

2. Seal and freeze.

TO ENJOY

Thaw the desired number of snack bags in the refrigerator.

My children love anything with pumpkin. So when our warehouse club began carrying canned pumpkin at prices far lower than at our grocery store, I knew it was time to get to work. When developing this recipe, I was aiming for a delicious muffin with extra fiber and calcium for my kids. The recipe does include butter, but the vitamin A, whole wheat flour, and added calcium make these muffins better than most commercial alternatives. —KN

PUMPKIN MUFFINS

MAKES APPROXIMATELY 3 DOZEN MUFFINS

3 cups all-purpose flour

3 cups whole wheat flour

2 cups packed brown sugar

1/3 cup dry milk powder (do not use instant)

2 tablespoons baking powder

1 tablespoon ground cinnamon

1 tablespoon cake spice (such as Penzeys, or try our handmade version on page 136)

1 teaspoon baking soda

1 (29-ounce) can pumpkin

1/2 cup (1 stick) butter, melted

6 eggs, beaten

2/3 cup milk

2 tablespoons double-strength vanilla extract

4 one-gallon freezer bags, labeled

1. Mix all-purpose flour, whole wheat flour, brown sugar, milk powder, baking powder, cinnamon, cake spice, and baking soda in a large bowl.

2. In a separate large bowl, using an electric mixer, mix pumpkin, melted butter, eggs, milk, and vanilla. Add the pumpkin mixture to the flour mixture, beating in half at a time until just combined. The batter will be stiff.

3. Preheat the oven to 375°F.

4. Grease three 12-cup regular muffin tins. (If you don't have enough muffin tins, bake the muffins in batches.) Fill each cup two-thirds full with batter. Bake for 20 to 25 minutes, or until a knife inserted into the center of a muffin comes out clean.

5. Allow muffins to cool for 3 to 5 minutes or until they are cool enough to handle. Transfer muffins to a cooling rack. Divide cooled muffins evenly among the freezer bags.

6. Seal and freeze.

TO ENJOY

1. Thaw desired number of muffins in the refrigerator.

2. Reheat in the microwave, in intervals of 10 to 15 seconds, until centers are warm.

DOUBLE VANILLA

You can find "double-fold" or "double-strength" pure vanilla at most grocery stores or from a variety of online retailers. If you can't find something to your liking, consider making your own vanilla extract. Add 2 or 3 vanilla beans to a quart of vodka, brandy, or rum, store in a cool, dark place, and you can begin curing your own extract.

This recipe is designed so you can go from zero to smoothie in no time flat. —LT

STRAWBERRY SMOOTHIES

MAKES 8 BATCHES, ABOUT 3 CUPS EACH

6 POUNDS FROZEN STRAWBERRIES

1 (32-ounce) container strawberry yogurt

1 pint orange juice concentrate

8 one-quart freezer bags, labeled

1. Divide strawberries evenly among the freezer bags. Into each bag, measure one ½ cup yogurt and ¼ cup orange juice concentrate.

2. Seal and freeze.

TO ENJOY

Thaw one bag in the refrigerator just enough to remove mix from bag. Put smoothie in a blender and add 1 cup cold water. Blend until smooth.

STAY COOL

If the smoothie thaws completely, simply blend with 1 cup ice.

Smoothies are great for a quick breakfast or a pick-me-up later in the day. Because the tropical fruit mix is naturally sweet, this recipe calls for plain yogurt. —LT

TROPICAL FRUIT SMOOTHIES

MAKES 8 BATCHES, ABOUT 3 CUPS EACH

**6 POUNDS FROZEN TROPI-
CAL FRUIT MIX**

1 (32-ounce) container plain yogurt

1 pint orange juice concentrate

8 one-quart freezer bags, labeled

1. Divide fruit evenly among the freezer bags. Into each bag, measure ½ cup yogurt and ¼ cup orange juice concentrate.

2. Seal and freeze.

TO ENJOY

Thaw one bag in the refrigerator just enough to remove mix from bag. Put smoothie in a blender and add 1 cup cold water. Blend until smooth.

Making healthful school lunches and after-school snacks can be a daily challenge. Kids, like adults, need variety in their diets, even if they complain about it. I try to make this mix more appealing by using high-quality white chocolate chips. In their August 2005 issue, *Cooks Illustrated* gave top tasting honors to the Guittard brand of white chocolate chips. Kids enjoy this mix straight from the bag and as a topping for tropical ice cream sundaes. —KN

BEACH DAY SNACK MIX

MAKES 6 SNACK BAGS

1½ cups dried banana chips
(6 ounces)

12 tablespoons chopped dried
mango (6 ounces)

12 tablespoons hulled sunflower
seeds

12 tablespoons shredded coconut
(3 ounces)

6 tablespoons white chocolate chips
(such as Guittard)

6 snack or sandwich bags

1 one-gallon freezer bag, labeled

1. Into each snack bag, place ¼ cup banana chips, 2 tablespoons mango, 2 tablespoons sunflower seeds, 2 tablespoons coconut, and 1 tablespoon white chocolate chips. Seal bags and gently shake to combine ingredients. Place all the snack bags into the 1-gallon freezer bag.

2. Seal and freeze.

TO ENJOY

Remove desired number of snack bags from freezer; thaw in refrigerator.

Here's another recipe I developed around a particular ingredient I wanted to try. These Asian-inspired treats offer a unique twist on a traditional butter cookie. —KN

FIVE-SPICE COOKIES

MAKES APPROXIMATELY 7 DOZEN COOKIES

2 cups (4 sticks) butter, softened

3 cups sugar

3 eggs

¼ cup milk

2 teaspoons orange extract

5½ cups all-purpose flour

2 tablespoons baking powder

½ teaspoon salt

7 one-quart freezer bags, labeled

TOPPING

½ cup sugar

2 teaspoons Chinese five-spice powder

ON HAND FOR BAKING

Parchment paper

1. Using an electric mixer, cream butter and sugar in a large bowl. Beat in eggs, milk, and orange extract. In a separate large bowl, mix flour, baking powder, and salt. Add half the flour mixture to the butter and egg mixture and beat well. Beat in remaining flour mixture.

2. In a small bowl, mix sugar and Chinese five-spice powder.

3. Roll dough into 1-inch balls. Roll dough balls in topping and place on a rimmed baking sheet.

4. Place in freezer for 30 minutes. Remove dough balls from freezer and place a dozen into each freezer bag.

5. Seal and freeze.

TO BAKE ONE DOZEN COOKIES

1. Place frozen cookies 3 inches apart on a parchment-lined baking sheet.

2. Preheat the oven to 375°F.

3. Bake for 8 to 10 minutes, or until tops crack.

4. Cool on baking sheet for 2 minutes; transfer to a cooling rack.

I don't want to make cookies from scratch as often as I want to eat them! I freeze the dough so I can bake fresh cookies at a moment's notice. This is a basic oatmeal cookie with a tropical twist. The dried coconut and mango make these cookies both crispy and chewy. —LT

OATMEAL COOKIES
WITH COCONUT AND MANGO

MAKES APPROXIMATELY 6 DOZEN COOKIES

2 cups (4 sticks) butter

2 cups packed brown sugar

2 eggs

2 teaspoons vanilla extract

3 cups all-purpose flour

3 cups old-fashioned rolled oats

1 cup unsweetened shredded coconut

1 cup chopped dried mango (8 ounces)

2 teaspoons baking powder

1 teaspoon baking soda

1 teaspoon salt

6 one-quart freezer bags, labeled

ON HAND FOR BAKING

Parchment paper

1. Using an electric mixer, cream butter, brown sugar, eggs, and vanilla in a large bowl. In a separate large bowl, mix flour, oats, coconut, mango, baking powder, baking soda, and salt. Add flour mixture to the butter mixture and stir well.

2. Refrigerate dough for 1 hour, or until firm enough to handle.

3. Roll dough into 1-inch balls and place on a rimmed baking sheet. Place in freezer for 30 minutes.

4. Remove dough balls from freezer. Place a dozen into each freezer bag.

5. Seal and freeze.

TO BAKE ONE DOZEN COOKIES

1. Completely thaw one bag in the refrigerator.

2. Preheat the oven to 350°F.

3. Place cookies 3 inches apart on a parchment-lined baking sheet. Flatten slightly with a fork. Bake for 14 to 16 minutes.

4. Cool on baking sheet for 2 minutes; transfer to a cooling rack.

PARCHMENT PAPER

We suggest parchment paper for our cookie recipes because it eliminates the need for greasing the baking sheet, which adds both a step and extra fat. The paper also makes moving the cookies a cinch — just lift the paper and transfer all the cookies to the cooling rack in one move.

These cookies are like gingersnaps, only without the snap — for the cookie lover who prefers soft, chewy cookies. Loaded with minced fresh ginger, this cookie is zingy and not too sweet. —LT

GINGER COOKIES

MAKES APPROXIMATELY 5 DOZEN COOKIES

1½ cups (3 sticks) butter

1½ cups packed brown sugar

½ cup molasses

¼ cup minced fresh ginger

2 eggs

4 cups all-purpose flour

1 tablespoon baking soda

5 one-quart freezer bags, labeled

1. Using an electric mixer, cream butter, brown sugar, molasses, ginger, and eggs in a large bowl. Add flour and baking soda and mix well.

2. Refrigerate dough for 1 hour, or until firm enough to handle.

3. Roll dough into 1-inch balls and place on a rimmed baking sheet. Place in freezer for 30 minutes.

4. Remove dough balls from freezer. Place a dozen into each freezer bag.

5. Seal and freeze.

TO BAKE ONE DOZEN COOKIES

1. Thaw one bag in the refrigerator or bake straight from the freezer.

2. Preheat the oven to 350°F.

3. Place cookies 3 inches apart on an ungreased baking sheet. Do not use parchment paper here. Do not flatten. Bake 15 to 17 minutes if frozen, 12 to 14 minutes if thawed.

4. Cool on baking sheet for 2 minutes; transfer to a cooling rack.

THE COOKIE SCOOP

A handy tool to use for any kind of rolled or drop cookie, a cookie scoop lets you skip refrigerating the dough before handling. If you've never used one, you've never experienced how fast cookie making can be! Unlike other kitchen gadgets that end up cluttering the drawer, this one really gets used. Cookie scoops can be found at your local kitchen retailer.

My family and I traveled to Sequim, Washington, one summer for its annual lavender festival. We toured several lavender farms, viewed acres of unique varietals, and enjoyed looking at the wares of local artists. I had fun observing the cornucopia of food and beverages made with fresh and dried lavender. My trip that day was the inspiration for these cookies. —KN

LEMON-LAVENDER BUTTER COOKIES

MAKES APPROXIMATELY 7 DOZEN COOKIES

2 cups (4 sticks) butter, softened

2½ cups granulated sugar

½ cup lavender sugar
(see Note at right)

3 eggs

¼ cup milk

2 teaspoons lemon extract

5½ cups all-purpose flour

2 tablespoons baking powder

½ teaspoon salt

7 one-quart freezer bags, labeled

TOPPING

½ cup lavender sugar

ON HAND FOR BAKING

Parchment paper

1. Using an electric mixer, cream butter, granulated sugar, and lavender sugar in a large bowl. Beat in eggs, milk, and lemon extract. In a separate large bowl, mix flour, baking powder, and salt. Add half the flour mixture to the butter and egg mixture and beat well. Beat in remaining flour mixture.

2. Roll dough into 1-inch balls. Pour topping into a small bowl. Roll dough balls in lavender sugar and place on a rimmed baking sheet.

3. Place in freezer for 30 minutes. Remove dough balls from freezer. Place a dozen into each freezer bag.

4. Seal and freeze.

TO BAKE ONE DOZEN COOKIES

1. Place frozen cookies 3 inches apart on a parchment-lined baking sheet.

2. Preheat the oven to 375°F.

3. Bake for 8 to 10 minutes, or until tops crack.

4. Cool on baking sheet for 2 minutes; transfer to a cooling rack.

LAVENDER SUGAR

It's cheaper to make your own lavender sugar than to buy it. Pour 1 cup sugar and 1 teaspoon (edible) lavender flowers into the bowl of a food processor. Process for 30 seconds. Remove any remaining large pieces of lavender by hand or pour sugar through a strainer. Cure the sugar in an airtight container at least 1 week before using.

These are a family favorite. The secret is high-quality, fresh cinnamon. If your cinnamon has been in the cupboard for years, replace it. Unless I have someone to share it with, ground cinnamon isn't something I buy at the warehouse — the containers are too large for my needs, and I hate to throw unused portions out. I buy cinnamon in smaller quantities, replacing old with new around Thanksgiving of each year, when I use it often in holiday baking. —KN

VERY VANILLA SNICKERDOODLES

MAKES APPROXIMATELY 7 DOZEN COOKIES

2 cups (4 sticks) butter, softened

3 cups sugar

3 eggs

¼ cup milk

2 teaspoons double-strength vanilla extract

3½ cups all-purpose flour

2 cups whole wheat flour

2 tablespoons baking powder

½ teaspoon salt

7 one-quart freezer bags, labeled

TOPPING

Scant ½ cup vanilla sugar (see Note at right)

1 tablespoon ground cinnamon

ON HAND FOR BAKING

Parchment paper

1. Using an electric mixer, cream butter and sugar in a large bowl. Beat in eggs, milk, and vanilla. In a separate large bowl, mix all-purpose flour, whole wheat flour, baking powder, and salt. Add half the flour mixture to the butter and egg mixture and beat well. Beat in remaining flour mixture. The batter will be stiff.

2. In a small bowl, mix sugar and cinnamon.

3. Roll the dough into 1-inch balls. Roll dough balls in topping and place on a rimmed baking sheet.

4. Place in freezer for 30 minutes.

5. Remove dough balls from freezer and place a dozen into each freezer bag.

6. Seal and freeze.

TO BAKE ONE DOZEN COOKIES

1. Place frozen cookies 3 inches apart on a parchment-lined baking sheet.

2. Preheat the oven to 375°F.

3. Bake for 8 to 10 minutes, or until tops crack. Cool on baking sheet for 2 minutes; transfer to a cooling rack.

VANILLA SUGAR

Making your own vanilla sugar is easy and inexpensive: Put 1 cup sugar and ¼ piece vanilla bean into the bowl of a food processor. Process for 30 to 60 seconds. Remove any remaining large pieces of vanilla by hand or pour sugar through a strainer. Cure the sugar in an airtight container at least 1 week before using.

BRANCHING OUT

ADAPTING YOUR OWN RECIPES FOR THE TRAY PACK METHOD

Once you've become experienced cooking with our method, there may come a time when you will want to adapt your own recipes for making ahead. Many of your favorite recipes will be good candidates for adaptation. Here are a few suggestions to consider:

CONSIDER THE MEAT. Look at the type and amount of meat in your original recipe. Be sure that the same or a similar cut of meat is sold at the warehouse. Divide the number of pounds in the club package by the amount required in your recipe. For example, if the original recipe calls for 1½ pounds of pork tenderloin, you take the warehouse package size of 4½ pounds and divide it by 1½, giving you the number 3. This tells you that you must multiply the recipe by 3 in order to use the entire package of pork. Begin with this general guideline, but expect to have to adjust individual recipe ingredients as discussed in the rest of this section.

ADJUST AMOUNTS FOR SALT AND PUNGENT SPICES. In our experience, many recipes call for too much salt in the first place. As a rule of thumb when doubling or tripling a recipe, the salt needs to be increased by only half. For example, if the original recipe calls for 1 teaspoon of salt, use ½ teaspoon for each factor of multiplication of the recipe. So, if you're doubling the recipe, you would use 1½ teaspoons of salt; for tripling, 2 teaspoons of salt total. Use this same rule of thumb for pungent spices, such as crushed red pepper, cinnamon, curry powder, cayenne pepper, and cumin. It's easier to add more seasoning to an underseasoned entrée than to diminish its effect after you've used too much.

BE CAREFUL WITH SALTY-FLAVORED SAUCES AND VINEGARS. Take care when multiplying salty sauces such as soy sauce, Worcestershire sauce, ketchup, and flavored vinegars. If you want to keep the same amount of liquid, consider using reduced-salt versions of these products, or use broth, apple juice, or water as a substitute for a portion of the original amount (see Firehouse Pork Skewers [page 127] as an example). If the amount of liquid is *not* a concern, begin by cutting the original amount called for by ⅓ before multiplying the ingredient.

MULTIPLY MILD HERBS AND SEASONINGS NORMALLY. Mild herbs and seasonings can be successfully multiplied without adjustment. Basil, oregano, thyme, marjoram, garlic, and ginger are not as concentrated as other spices. It's still possible to use too much, but the probability that too much of these seasonings will ruin an entire batch of entrées is low.

TAKE NOTES AS YOU EXPERIMENT. Good record keeping will help you perfect a recipe you're adapting. Sometimes, the right amount of sauce, marinade, breading, or topping for one recipe will be too much or too little when multiplied for several recipes. Take notes while you're putting a recipe together, and after you've eaten the dish, too, so you'll know what to adjust the next time.

REMEMBER THAT CERTAIN INGREDIENTS, SUCH AS LETTUCE AND CUCUMBERS, DO NOT FREEZE SUCCESSFULLY. Other ingredients need special care before they go into the freezer: for example, raw potato will turn black in the freezer, so be sure to cook it first. Some vegetables freeze fine when raw as long as they're in a sauce or soup (carrots and celery, for example), but others should be blanched before freezing (cauliflower and green beans). See resources (page 241) for books that discuss freezing vegetables, fruits, and herbs in more detail.

COMMUNITY COOKING OPTIONS: FOOD AS FELLOWSHIP

Many of the recipes in *Fix, Freeze, Feast* were developed while we were operating our own in-home meal-preparation businesses. Our businesses were a little different from the do-it-yourself group because we planned, shopped, and organized all the details for each group. Yet the recipes we developed lend themselves nicely to the small group that wishes to begin cooking together on its own. Cooking groups have been featured in many magazines and on popular Internet sites because they're a great option for individuals who want to save time and money while enjoying the company of friends. What could be better? There are several ways to structure a do-it-yourself cooking group:

A COOKING CLUB. In a cooking club, the group agrees on what recipes to make, divides the shopping and organizing duties, and comes together on a specified day to prepare the meals *together*. This arrangement works well for members who have different skills and task preferences. For example, a person who dislikes shopping but doesn't mind dealing with money will probably be happy in a group with someone who loves shopping but dislikes money matters. It also works well for groups whose members don't want to go back home alone to cook in their own kitchens but have time for and are open to a more social experience of meeting new members and catching up with friends. The home party is our specialty. For more information and how-tos for home parties, visit our Web site *www.fixfreezefeast.com.*

A COOKING CO-OP. In a co-op format the group assigns recipes to individuals. Members go home and make their entrées and everyone meets later to swap meals. Each person is responsible for shopping and cooking all entrées of the assigned recipe. For example, in a cooking group of six, if Sue gets assigned Beef Barley Soup and Jenny gets Sweet Asian Chicken, each will make six of their assigned recipe and then meet at a designated spot to swap. At the swap, each member gives five entrées away and receives five from the other members. The cooking co-op format works well for groups that have difficulty finding the time or space to gather for food preparation and cooking.

Whatever type of group cooking you choose — a club, a co-op, or a hybrid of the two — the benefits of cooking together remain the same. Together you share the costs, in time and money. Together you try new dishes without doing all the recipe research, planning, and work. And, perhaps most important, you get to do it all with friends, supporting one another, exploring new foods, and building relationships along the way.

FOOD AS SERVICE

Put your experience with make-ahead meals to good use for charity. The skills you've developed with this method could be used to make a wonderful donation to a nonprofit group. Schools, community service agencies, and religious organizations often need donations for auctions and other fund-raisers. A selection of frozen entrées garners high bids — everyone wants make-ahead meals!

FOOD AS MINISTRY

When a friend or neighbor is facing a crisis or transition, a practical way to help is by providing a meal or two. People often offer their good intentions: "Let me know if there's anything I can do to help," but the person in crisis is then placed in the awkward position of having to ask for help. Even the most organized, accomplished cook may find it difficult to continue with regular tasks when faced with a major disruption in the regular routine. If you show up with some frozen entrées in hand, you'll have the satisfaction of helping and your friend will appreciate your thoughtfulness.

Keeping meals on hand means needs can be met as they arise, not just when you have some extra time. Often meals are needed in a hurry, such as when there is a death, a sudden illness, or another unexpected trauma. Other times, the provision of meals can be planned for, as in the case of a scheduled surgery or a baby's birth or adoption. It won't take long before you begin to see needs all around you that can easily be met with make-ahead meals.

Structured ways of providing meals within communities exist, too. In many churches, support groups, and other groups of like-minded people, meal banks are becoming a popular way to keep nutritious food on hand for those in need. Small groups can gather to prepare entrées to be stored in a church or community freezer and delivered at the necessary time. The meal bank can be set up formally with set times for filling the freezer and specific people in charge of delivery, or it can be done more casually to supplement an existing hot meal delivery program.

Whether you want to explore this idea on your own or with a group, here are some things to keep in mind when considering recipe selection:

CHOOSE FOR FLAVOR. It's best to choose recipes that are middle of the road on heat and spices. Children, the elderly, nursing mothers, and those who are ill may be more sensitive to spicy foods. This doesn't mean you have to eliminate recipes for such dishes from the menu; just leave out the crushed red pepper, cayenne pepper, or hot pepper sauce. Other good recipe choices are those that are classic, family-friendly fare. Choose entrées that will have the widest appeal.

CHOOSE FOR EASE OF PREPARATION. You never know who might be preparing the entrée on the other end — perhaps a spouse or a teenager who has little experience in the kitchen. Make no assumptions about cooking abilities; select entrées that are easily baked or reheated. Unless you're certain a person has, say, a slow cooker, you will want to avoid recipes that require that method of cooking.

CHOOSE FOR VARIETY. When preparing entrées to hold as inventory, it's wise to have some selections for vegetarians, those with dairy allergies, and those who have fat, sugar, or salt restrictions. There's no need for a huge selection of items — just plan to have enough selections to meet the needs of a variety of potential recipients.

CHOOSE FOR COST. Maximize your budget by selecting recipes with less-expensive cuts of meat and those that can be stretched by serving the dish over rice or noodles. Recipes that use meat in smaller proportions, such as for soup, chili, or meatballs, are also good choices.

CHOOSE FOR MORE THAN JUST DINNER. People appreciate receiving breakfast, lunch, and snack items just as much as dinner entrées.

PACKAGING

Always consider the needs of the recipient when you are packaging meals for others. It can be problematic for someone to keep track of containers that need to be returned. Unless you are certain that the recipient would prefer otherwise, package the meals in freezer bags, plastic containers, or foil pans, and let the recipient know that you don't expect to get them back.

Finally, if you've ever been the recipient of a meal when your life was turned upside down, you already know what a difference it can make. Until you have experienced it yourself, it may seem like an insignificant way to help. But to the mom who has had a sleepless night with her new baby or to a family grieving the death of a loved one, a meal can be a lifeline. More than just nourishment for the body, it is one way to connect us as a community.

Frozen Gifts: A hot meal is helpful, but frozen meals are more versatile. It can be a lifesaver to have a meal in the freezer several weeks after a life-changing event.

APPENDIXES

SAMPLE SHOPPING LIST

BASIL-BALSAMIC CHOPS
BERRY-ROASTED CHICKEN (INCLUDING HANDMADE RASPBERRY VINAIGRETTE)
4 Bs FLANK STEAK

WAREHOUSE CLUB

1 tray pork loin chops

1 two-pack whole chickens

1 tray flank steak

1 cup (1 medium) chopped onion

3 + 2 teaspoons minced garlic

1 + 1 cup olive oil

$\frac{1}{2}$ cup red wine vinegar

2 + 1 tablespoons honey

$\frac{1}{4}$ cup soy sauce

$\frac{1}{4}$ cup lemon juice

$\frac{1}{4}$ cup Dijon mustard

$\frac{1}{2}$ + $\frac{1}{4}$ cup + 1 tablespoon balsamic vinegar

$2\frac{1}{4}$ + $\frac{1}{2}$ + $\frac{1}{2}$ + $\frac{1}{4}$ teaspoons black pepper

3 + 2 + 2 one-gallon freezer bags

GROCERY STORE

$1\frac{1}{2}$ cups Black Butte Porter

$\frac{1}{2}$ cup ketchup

1 teaspoon spicy brown mustard

3 teaspoons dried basil

$\frac{1}{2}$ + $\frac{1}{2}$ teaspoon salt

2 cups (12 ounces) frozen mixed berries

$\frac{1}{2}$ cup fresh or frozen raspberries

$\frac{1}{4}$ cup dark brown sugar

Go through each recipe and note on the shopping list the amount of each ingredient you'll need. Once your list is complete, check to be sure you've included everything. It's easier to double-check each recipe's ingredients if they're listed separately. For example, list 3 + 2 + 2 one-gallon freezer bags rather than the total of 7.

Set up two columns, one for the warehouse club and one for the grocery store. Place the ingredient in the column where you most often buy the item.

If you know you have the item on hand, list it anyway. You will place a check mark by it before you go shopping. It's best to have it on the list so you have a reference for everything you need for the cooking session.

Separate columns by area of the store (meat, produce, dairy) and you'll avoid backtracking inside the store.

On a recent trip to the warehouse to buy ingredients for Mango-Cranberry Chicken, I discovered the store was sold out of boneless, skinless chicken breast. Although this rarely happens, I was prepared to change my plan since I had the pages of this book along. I settled on Cam's Ribs instead and was able to leave the store with everything I needed. —LT

SAMPLE PREP LIST

BASIL-BALSAMIC CHOPS
BERRY-ROASTED CHICKEN (INCLUDING HANDMADE RASPBERRY VINAIGRETTE)
4 Bs FLANK STEAK

- mince garlic — 5 teaspoons
- chop onion — 1 cup
- make Raspberry Vinaigrette
- label bags

Once you prepare these items, you can follow the recipes as written. This is an easy prep list because it involves some of our simplest recipes. A prep list might be longer and more involved if the recipes have more vegetables or sauces to prepare.

STANDARD WAREHOUSE CLUB TRAY PACKS

CHICKEN

BONELESS, SKINLESS CHICKEN HALF-BREASTS: One tray weighs about 6 pounds and typically contains 12 half-breasts.

BONELESS, SKINLESS CHICKEN THIGHS: One tray weighs about 6 pounds and typically contains 20 thighs.

CHICKEN THIGHS ON THE BONE: One tray weighs about 7 pounds and typically contains 16 pieces.

WHOLE CHICKENS: Two individually wrapped birds are sold in one package, which typically weighs 8–10 pounds.

PORK

PORK TENDERLOIN: One tray weighs about $4\frac{1}{2}$ pounds.

PORK LOIN: This cut is sold as individual shrink-wrapped loins of varying sizes. Our recipes call for 8-pound loins. Do not choose the rolled and tied pork loin roast for our recipes.

PORK LOIN CHOPS, BONELESS OR BONE-IN: One tray weighs 6–8 pounds and typically contains 10–15 chops, depending on which cut you choose. Our recipes call for 12 chops.

BONELESS COUNTRY-STYLE RIBS: These trays vary in size. Our recipes call for 8-pound packages.

BEEF

GROUND BEEF: One tray weighs about 6 pounds.

FLANK STEAK: One tray weighs about 3 pounds and contains 2 large steaks.

BONELESS TOP SIRLOIN STEAK: One tray weighs about 6 pounds and contains 4 large steaks.

SIRLOIN TIP BEEF ROAST: This cut is sold as individual shrink-wrapped roasts of varying sizes. Our recipes call for 6-pound roasts.

FREEZER INVENTORY

Record the recipe title and date prepared, and circle when you place in freezer: (in)/ out

When you remove a recipe from the freezer, circle "out": (in)/ (out)

Items are best used within three months of freezing unless otherwise noted in the recipe itself.

Recipe	Date Prepared	In/Out			
		in/out	in/out	in/out	in/out
		in/out	in/out	in/out	in/out
		in/out	in/out	in/out	in/out
		in/out	in/out	in/out	in/out
		in/out	in/out	in/out	in/out
		in/out	in/out	in/out	in/out
		in/out	in/out	in/out	in/out
		in/out	in/out	in/out	in/out
		in/out	in/out	in/out	in/out
		in/out	in/out	in/out	in/out
		in/out	in/out	in/out	in/out
		in/out	in/out	in/out	in/out
		in/out	in/out	in/out	in/out
		in/out	in/out	in/out	in/out
		in/out	in/out	in/out	in/out
		in/out	in/out	in/out	in/out
		in/out	in/out	in/out	in/out
		in/out	in/out	in/out	in/out
		in/out	in/out	in/out	in/out
		in/out	in/out	in/out	in/out
		in/out	in/out	in/out	in/out
		in/out	in/out	in/out	in/out
		in/out	in/out	in/out	in/out

FREEZER LABELS *Copy these cooking instructions onto labels for your frozen food packages, or simply copy and tape onto your freezer bags.*

CHERRY SKILLET CHICKEN

Completely thaw entreé in the refrigerator. Heat 2 teaspoons vegetable oil in a large skillet over medium heat. Add the chicken and cook until it begins to brown, about 3 minutes on each side. Reduce heat to medium-low and pour cherries and juice over chicken. Cover and simmer 12 to 15 minutes, or until an instant-read thermometer inserted into the thickest part of the chicken reads 170°F.

CHICKEN CURRY

Completely thaw entrée in the refrigerator. In a large skillet over medium heat, bring the chicken and curry sauce to a simmer and cook until heated through. Do not boil.

CHICKEN-BROCCOLI BAKE

Completely thaw entrée in the refrigerator. Place chicken and broccoli mixture in an ungreased baking dish and sprinkle with cheese and breadcrumbs. Bake, uncovered, at 350°F for 35 to 40 minutes, or until the sauce is bubbling and the cheese is melted.

CHICKEN PARMIGIANA

Completely thaw entrée in the refrigerator. Place chicken in a greased baking dish. Bake, uncovered, at 375°F for 20 minutes. Pour red sauce evenly over each piece of chicken and continue baking for 10 minutes longer, or until an instant-read thermometer inserted into the thickest part of the chicken reads 170°F. Place a slice of cheese on top of each piece of chicken and bake until melted.

CHICKEN CORDON BLEU

Remove desired number of chicken rolls from freezer. Discard plastic wrap while chicken is still frozen and place rolls in a greased baking dish. Place in the refrigerator to thaw completely. Brush each chicken roll with 2 teaspoons melted butter and bake at 350°F for 45 minutes, or until an instant read thermometer inserted into the thickest part of the chicken reads 170°F.

DAVE'S SWAMP BLUES BARBECUED CHICKEN

Completely thaw entrée in the refrigerator. Prepare a medium-low fire in a gas or charcoal grill. Cook chicken, turning every 5 minutes and basting frequently, for 30 minutes, or until an instant-read thermometer inserted into the thickest part of the chicken reads 170°F. Do not baste chicken during last 5 minutes of grilling.

MARIACHI CHICKEN ROLLS

Completely thaw entrée in the refrigerator. Remove foil and plastic wrap from dish and replace foil. Bake, covered, at 350°F for 1 hour, or until an instant-read thermometer inserted into the center of a roll reads 170°F.

PECAN-CRUSTED CHICKEN STRIPS

Completely thaw entrée in the refrigerator. Place pecans/breadcrumbs on a plate. Shake excess sauce off each piece of chicken, roll in crumbs, and place on a greased baking sheet. Bake at 350°F for 30 minutes, or until chicken pulls apart easily and is no longer pink in the thickest part, and crust is golden.

MANGO-CRANBERRY CHICKEN

Completely thaw entrée in the refrigerator. Simmer chicken and sauce in a large skillet over medium-high heat until meat is thoroughly cooked, 15 to 20 minutes. Serve hot over rice or noodles.

PORT BARBECUED CHICKEN

Completely thaw entrée in the refrigerator. Prepare a medium-low fire in a gas or charcoal grill. Cook chicken, turning every 5 minutes and basting frequently, for 30 minutes, or until an instant-read thermometer inserted into the thickest part of the chicken reads 170°F. Do not baste chicken during last 5 minutes of grilling. Boil remaining sauce for at least 5 minutes if you wish to serve it with the chicken.

MOLASSES-RUM CHICKEN

Completely thaw entrée in the refrigerator. Prepare a medium-low fire in a gas or charcoal grill. Cook chicken, turning occasionally, for 30 minutes, or until an instant-read thermometer inserted into the thickest part of the chicken reads 170°F. Discard remaining marinade.

CHICKEN ROLLS WITH CRISPY ALMOND/RYE BREADING

Remove rolls from freezer and place in a greased 9-inch square baking dish. Cover and place in the refrigerator to thaw completely. Bake, uncovered, at 350°F for 45 to 60 minutes, or until an instant-read thermometer inserted into the thickest part of a roll reads 170°F.

SWEET ASIAN CHICKEN

Completely thaw entrée in the refrigerator. Prepare a medium-low fire in a gas or charcoal grill. Cook chicken, turning every 5 minutes and basting frequently, for 30 minutes, or until an instant-read thermometer inserted into the thickest part of the chicken reads 170°F. Do not baste chicken during last 5 minutes of grilling. Discard remaining marinade. *See main recipe for indoor cooking instructions.*

TEQUILA-LIME CHICKEN

Completely thaw entrée in the refrigerator. Prepare a medium-low fire in a gas or charcoal grill. Cook chicken, turning every 5 minutes and basting frequently, for 30 minutes, or until an instant-read thermometer inserted into the thickest part of the chicken reads 170°F. Do not baste chicken during last 5 minutes of grilling. Discard remaining marinade. *See main recipe for indoor cooking instructions.*

SWIMMING RAMA

Completely thaw entrée in the refrigerator. In a large skillet over medium heat, bring the chicken and sauce to a simmer and cook until heated through. Do not boil. To serve, place a handful of fresh spinach leaves on each plate. Top with a generous serving of chicken and sauce. Pass hot steamed rice.

CASHEW CHICKEN STIR-FRY

Needed on hand to complete this entrée: ½ pound assorted fresh stir-fry vegetables; 2 teaspoons sesame oil. Completely thaw entrée in the refrigerator. Heat oil in a large skillet over medium-high heat and stir-fry chicken and sauce until meat is almost cooked through, 20 minutes. Add vegetables; stir-fry until tender crisp. Sprinkle with cashews and serve.

TEX-MEX CHICKEN FINGERS

Completely thaw entrée in the refrigerator. Bake chicken fingers on a greased baking sheet at 350°F for 30 minutes, or until chicken pulls apart easily and is no longer pink in the center of the thickest part..

PEANUT SATAY

Needed on hand to complete this entrée: 8 (9-inch) skewers. Completely thaw entrée in the refrigerator. If using wooden skewers, soak them in water. Thread chicken pieces onto skewers. Prepare a medium-low fire in a gas or charcoal grill. Grill until chicken pulls apart easily and is no longer pink in the center of the thickest part. Discard remaining marinade. *See main recipe for indoor cooking instructions.*

HONEY-GLAZED CHICKEN THIGHS

Thaw entrée in the refrigerator just long enough to remove from the freezer bag. Place frozen chicken in an ungreased baking dish. Bake at 350°F for 45 minutes. Remove dish from oven, separate chicken pieces, and place them meaty side down. Bake for 1½ hours longer, or until an instant read thermometer inserted into the thickest part of the chicken reads 180°F and the sauce has browned and is thick and sticky.

ROYAL THAI THIGHS

Completely thaw entrée in the refrigerator. Bake, uncovered, at 375°F for 45 minutes, or until an instant-read thermometer inserted into the thickest part of the chicken reads 180°F.

TERIYAKI CHICKEN

Completely thaw entrée in the refrigerator. Place chicken in an ungreased baking dish. Bake, uncovered, at 350°F for 1 hour, or until an instant-read thermometer inserted into the thickest part of the chicken reads 180°F. Turn pieces once or twice during baking. The longer the cooking time, the thicker and stickier the sauce will be.

BERRY-ROASTED CHICKEN

Completely thaw one bag of chicken in the refrigerator. Place chicken, breast side up, in a greased baking dish and pour marinade into cavity. Roast at 325°F for about 1½ hours, or until an instant-read thermometer inserted into the thigh reads 180°F. Garnish with raspberries, if desired.

SWEET CHICKEN TOSTADA FILLING

Completely thaw one bag of filling in the refrigerator. Bring the filling to a simmer in a large skillet over medium-low heat. Do not boil. Use as a filling for tacos, tostadas, or burritos.

CHICKEN À LA KING

Completely thaw entrée in the refrigerator. Simmer the chicken and sauce in a large skillet over medium heat until warmed through. Do not boil.

MEDITERRANEAN ROAST CHICKEN

Completely thaw one bag of chicken in the refrigerator. Place chicken, breast side up, in a greased baking dish. Surround chicken with olives, capers, and marinade. Add just enough water to cover the bottom of the baking dish. Roast at 325°F for about 1½ hours, or until an instant-read thermometer inserted into the thigh reads 180°F.

URBAN GARLIC CHICKEN

Completely thaw entrée in the refrigerator. Place chicken, breast side up, in a greased baking dish. Put carrot, celery, and onion in cavity. Roast at 325°F for about 1½ hours, or until an instant-read thermometer inserted into the thigh reads 180°F.

MINI CHICKEN POTPIE

Needed on hand to complete this entrée: 12 slices of sandwich bread, cut into 3½-inch circles. Completely thaw one bag of filling in the refrigerator. Gently press bread rounds into a greased 12-cup regular muffin tin so that the bottom and sides are covered. The bread may not go all the way to the top of each form. Toast bread in the oven 8 to 10 minutes, or to desired firmness and color. While bread is toasting, bring the chicken to a simmer in a medium saucepan. Do not boil. Remove toasted bread cups from muffin tin. Fill each bread cup with chicken filling and serve.

PARTY ENCHILADAS

Completely thaw one dish in the refrigerator. Remove plastic wrap and foil and replace foil. Bake, covered, at 350°F for 25 minutes. Remove foil and bake 5 to 10 minutes longer, or until sauce is bubbling.

BEEF AND BEAN BURRITOS

Thaw the burritos in the refrigerator or reheat them straight from the freezer.
Microwave: Remove foil, defrost, and reheat.
Oven: Bake in foil at 375°F for 30 minutes if frozen, 300°F for 30 minutes if thawed.

CHEESY CHILADA BAKE

Completely thaw one dish in the refrigerator. Remove plastic wrap and foil from baking dish and replace foil. Bake at 350°F for 40 minutes, or until center is hot and edges are bubbly.

HABANERO AND CHILI HAMBURGERS

Remove patties from the freezer. Place on a plate and completely thaw in the refrigerator. Prepare a medium-low fire in a gas or charcoal grill. Cook burgers 5 to 6 minutes per side, or until an instant-read thermometer inserted into the thickest part of the patty reads 160°F. *See main recipe for indoor cooking instructions.*

CLASSIC LASAGNA: LARGE PAN

Thaw entrée in the refrigerator or bake it straight from the freezer. Remove plastic wrap and foil from baking dish and replace foil. Place dish on a rimmed baking sheet and bake at 375°F for 1 hour if thawed, 1½ hours if frozen. Remove foil and continue baking until lasagna is bubbling and cheese is browned.

SPANISH RICE

Completely thaw entrée in the refrigerator. Put meat and rice mixture in an ungreased baking dish and sprinkle with the cheese. Bake, covered, at 350°F for 30 to 40 minutes, or until sauce is bubbling and cheese is melted.

CLASSIC LASAGNA: SMALL PAN

Thaw entrée in the refrigerator or bake it straight from the freezer. Remove plastic wrap and foil from baking dish and replace foil. Bake at 375°F for 45 minutes if thawed, 1 hour if frozen. Remove foil and continue baking until lasagna is bubbling and cheese is browned.

MEXI-STUFFED PEPPERS

Completely thaw entrée in the refrigerator. Prepare peppers for stuffing: wash, cut off tops, and seed peppers. Fill each with meat mixture. Sprinkle tops with cheese. Place on a greased rimmed baking sheet. Bake at 350°F for 35 minutes, or until filling is hot.

MOZZARELLA MEATBALLS

Completely thaw entrée in the refrigerator. Pour meatballs and sauce into an ungreased baking dish. Bake, uncovered, at 350°F for 30 minutes, or until meatballs are heated through. Serve over rice.

CLASSIC CHILI

Completely thaw entrée in the refrigerator. Cook, stirring occasionally, in a medium saucepan over low heat for 1 hour, or until liquid cooks off and chili is thick.

SALISBURY MEATBALLS

Completely thaw entrée in the refrigerator. Prepare on the stove or in the oven.

STOVE TOP: Bring meatballs and sauce to a simmer in a large skillet over medium heat until meatballs are heated through. Do not boil.

OVEN: Pour meatballs and sauce into an ungreased baking dish. Bake, uncovered, at 350°F for 30 minutes, or until meatballs are heated through. Serve over rice, mashed potatoes, or noodles.

4 Bs FLANK STEAK

Completely thaw entrée in the refrigerator. Prepare a medium fire in a gas or charcoal grill. Cook steak 15 to 20 minutes for medium-rare to medium. Turn occasionally and baste as desired. Do not baste during final 5 minutes of cooking. Discard remaining marinade.

SWEET-AND-SOUR MEATBALLS

Completely thaw entrée in refrigerator. Prepare in the oven or a slow cooker.

OVEN: Put meatballs and sauce in an ungreased baking dish and bake, uncovered, at 350°F for 30 minutes, or until meatballs are heated through.

SLOW COOKER: Put meatballs and sauce in a slow cooker. Cook on low for 2 to 5 hours, or until meatballs are heated through.

BLACKJACK STEAK

Completely thaw entrée in the refrigerator. Prepare a medium fire in a gas or charcoal grill. Cook steak 15 to 20 minutes for medium-rare to medium. Turn occasionally and baste as desired. Do not baste during final 5 minutes of cooking. Discard remaining marinade.

ROSE CITY TERIYAKI

Completely thaw entrée in the refrigerator. Prepare a medium fire in a gas or charcoal grill. Cook steak 15 to 20 minutes for medium-rare to medium. Turn occasionally and baste as desired. Do not baste during final 5 minutes of cooking. Discard remaining marinade.

SESAME-SOY SIRLOIN

Completely thaw entrée in the refrigerator. Prepare a medium fire in a gas or charcoal grill. Cook steak 14 to 18 minutes for medium-rare to medium. Turn occasionally and baste as desired. Do not baste during final 5 minutes of cooking. Discard remaining marinade.

BEEF FAJITAS

Needed on hand to complete this entrée: 2 teaspoons vegetable oil. Completely thaw entrée in the refrigerator. Heat oil in a large skillet over medium-high heat. Add onions and peppers; stir-fry until soft, about 3 minutes. Remove vegetables from skillet; add beef. Stir-fry until well browned, about 10 minutes. Remove pan from heat and return vegetables, stirring to combine. Serve with your favorite toppings.

BEEF BARLEY SOUP

Put frozen soup into slow cooker. (Soup doesn't need to be thawed.) Add 4 cups of water and the bag of barley. Cook on low for 8 to 10 hours or on high for 4 to 5 hours, or until the meat and vegetables are tender.

SHANGHAI STIR-FRY

Needed on hand to complete this entrée: 2 teaspoons vegetable oil; 1 (11-ounce) can mandarin orange slices, drained; 2 teaspoons sesame seeds. Completely thaw entrée in the refrigerator. Pour off the marinade and reserve. Heat oil in a large skillet over medium-high heat. Add beef and stir-fry until well browned, about 10 minutes. Remove beef from pan and keep warm. Add marinade to skillet, reduce-heat, and simmer for 3 minutes. Return beef to pan. Add mandarin oranges and stir to coat. Serve over rice. Sprinkle with sesame seeds.

STEAK SKEWERS WITH BLUE CHEESE DIPPING SAUCE

Needed on hand to complete this entrée: 8 (9-inch) skewers. Completely thaw entrée in the refrigerator. If using wooden skewers, soak them in water while beef is thawing. Thread steak pieces onto skewers. Prepare a medium fire in a gas or charcoal grill. Grill, turning occasionally, about 10 minutes or until beef is done to your liking. Discard remaining marinade. Meanwhile, heat the blue cheese mixture in a medium saucepan over medium heat. Simmer gently, stirring frequently, until the cream reduces and thickens into a velvety sauce, about 40 minutes. Serve as a dipping sauce with the steak skewers. See main recipe for indoor cooking instructions.

CHEESE STEAKS

Needed on hand to complete this entrée: 2 teaspoons vegetable oil; foil. Thaw entrée in the refrigerator or cook it straight from the freezer. Put beef and broth into slow cooker. Cook on low for 5 to 6 hours, or until the beef is tender and pulls apart easily with a fork. Remove beef from broth and set aside until cool enough to shred. Reserve broth. Meanwhile, heat oil in a large skillet over medium-high heat. Add peppers and onions and stir-fry until soft, about 3 minutes. Remove pan from heat. Slice and open rolls. Divide beef and vegetables evenly among the rolls. Place a slice of cheese inside each sandwich; close and wrap in foil. Heat in the oven at 350°F for 10 minutes. Unwrap carefully. Serve with broth for dipping.

GINGER BEEF

Thaw entrée in the refrigerator or cook it straight from the freezer. Put beef and broth into slow cooker. Cook on low for 5 to 6 hours, or until beef is fork tender.

4 Bs GRILLED CHOPS

Completely thaw entrée in the refrigerator. Prepare a medium-low fire in a gas or charcoal grill. Cook chops until an instant-read thermometer inserted into the thickest part of a chop reads 160°F. Discard remaining marinade.

AN'S PORK CHOPS

Completely thaw entrée in the refrigerator. Prepare a medium-low fire in a gas or charcoal grill. Cook chops until an instant-read thermometer inserted into the thickest part of a chop reads 160°F. Discard remaining marinade.

CAJUN BRAISED SKILLET CHOPS

Completely thaw entrée in the refrigerator. Heat 1½ tablespoons oil in a deep skillet over medium heat. Fry chops 3 minutes on each side; remove from pan. Pour broth and vegetables into pan. Gently scrape browned bits from the bottom; reduce heat to medium-low. Return chops to pan. Simmer, covered, 15 to 20 minutes, or until an instant-read thermometer inserted into the thickest part of a chop reads 160°F.

PEPPER JELLY PORK CHOPS

Completely thaw entrée in the refrigerator. Prepare a medium fire in a gas or charcoal grill. Cook chops, turning occasionally, until an instant-read thermometer inserted into the thickest part of a chop reads 160°F. Discard remaining marinade. *See main recipe for indoor cooking instructions.*

MARGARITA PORK CHOPS

Completely thaw entrée in the refrigerator. Prepare a medium fire in a gas or charcoal grill. Cook chops, turning occasionally, until an instant-read thermometer inserted into the thickest part of a chop reads 160°F. Discard remaining marinade. *See main recipe for indoor cooking instructions.*

BASIL-BALSAMIC CHOPS

Completely thaw entrée in the refrigerator. Prepare a medium fire in a gas or charcoal grill. Cook chops, turning occasionally, until an instant-read thermometer inserted into the thickest part of a chop reads 160°F. Discard remaining marinade. *See main recipe for indoor cooking instructions.*

MUSTARD-OREGANO CHOPS

Completely thaw entrée in the refrigerator. Prepare a medium fire in a gas or charcoal grill. Cook chops, turning occasionally, until an instant-read thermometer inserted into the thickest part of a chop reads 160°F. Discard remaining marinade. *See main recipe for indoor cooking instructions.*

TURKISH PORK LOIN CHOPS WITH BACON

Place chops in an ungreased baking dish. Cover and completely thaw in the refrigerator. Bake chops, uncovered, at 350°F for 45 to 60 minutes, or until an instant-read thermometer inserted into the thickest part of a chop reads 160°F. **Note:** Two to four chops will fit nicely in a 9- by 9-inch baking dish. If cooking five or more chops, use a 13- by 9-inch baking dish.

CAM'S RIBS

Completely thaw entrée in the refrigerator. Place the ribs in a large stockpot and cover with water. Set bag of sauce aside. Simmer ribs about 1 hour, or until tender. Drain ribs and place in an ungreased baking dish. Pour sauce over ribs. Bake, uncovered, basting ribs with sauce every 10 minutes, at 350°F for 1 hour.

STICKY RIBS

Completely thaw entrée in the refrigerator. Place the ribs in a large stockpot and cover with water. Set bag of sauce aside. Simmer ribs about 1 hour, or until tender. Drain ribs and place in an ungreased baking dish. Pour sauce over ribs. Bake, uncovered, at 350°F for about 1 hour or until sauce is thick and sticky.

FIREHOUSE PORK SKEWERS

Needed on hand to complete this entrée: 1 medium onion, cut into 8 wedges; 10–12 (9-inch) skewers. Completely thaw entrée in the refrigerator. If using wooden skewers, soak them in water while meat is thawing. Thread pork pieces and onion onto skewers. Prepare a medium fire in a gas or charcoal grill. Cook 12 to 15 minutes, turning occasionally. Discard remaining marinade.

CARIBBEAN PORK TENDERLOIN

Completely thaw entrée in the refrigerator. Prepare a medium-low fire in a gas or charcoal grill. Cook tenderloin until an instant-read thermometer inserted into the thickest part of the pork reads 160°F. Discard remaining marinade.

APPLE AND CRANBERRY PORK LOIN

Completely thaw entrée in the refrigerator. Place roast in the center of an ungreased baking dish, distributing apples and onions around roast. Bake, uncovered, at 350°F for 1 hour, or until an instant-read thermometer inserted into the thickest part of the roast reads 160°F.

PORK LOIN WITH APRICOT/SAUSAGE STUFFING

Needed on hand to complete this entrée: ½ cup sour cream. Completely thaw entrée in the refrigerator. Stuff roast pocket with the apricot and sausage mixture. Place roast in an ungreased baking dish. Spread sauce over the roast, covering completely. Bake, uncovered, at 350°F for 45 to 60 minutes, or until an instant-read thermometer inserted into the stuffing and the thickest part of the roast reads 160°F. When roast is done, transfer drippings to a small saucepan and simmer until liquid reduces by about half. Stir in ¼ cup sour cream and spoon over pork slices.

AUSTRIAN PORK GOULASH

Completely thaw entrée in the refrigerator. Put pork and onion mixture in a large stockpot and add 1½ cups water. Cook goulash over medium heat until pork is completely cooked through and sauce has thickened, 30 to 40 minutes. Add more water during cooking if goulash becomes dry. Serve over hot rice.

PORK LOIN RAGOUT

Completely thaw entrée in the refrigerator. Put onion and pepper mixture into slow cooker. Put roast and sauce on top. Cook on low for 8 to 10 hours. Remove bay leaves. Shred cooked pork with a fork, mix with the sauce, and serve over pasta.

PORK RAGOUT LASAGNA

Completely thaw entrée in the refrigerator. Remove plastic wrap and foil from baking dish and replace foil. Bake at 375°F for 50 minutes. Remove foil and continue baking 20 to 30 minutes longer, or until center is hot and the cheeses are browned. Remove from oven and let stand for 10 minutes before serving. **Note:** This lasagna can be cooked without freezing; however, allow it to sit in the refrigerator for a day or more so that the noodles absorb liquid and soften before baking.

HONEY AND SPICE PORK KABOBS

Needed on hand to complete this entrée: 10–12 (9-inch) skewers. Completely thaw entrée in the refrigerator. If using wooden skewers, soak them in water while meat is thawing. Thread pork pieces onto skewers. Prepare a medium-low fire in a gas or charcoal grill. Cook 15 to 18 minutes, turning occasionally and basting as desired, until thoroughly cooked. Do not baste during final 5 minutes of cooking. Discard remaining marinade.

RAGING GARLIC PORK STIR-FRY

Needed on hand to complete this entrée: 2 teaspoons vegetable oil, ½ cup cornstarch. Completely thaw entrée in the refrigerator. Pour off and discard any excess liquid from the bag of pork. Add cornstarch; seal bag and shake to coat. Heat oil in a large skillet over medium-high heat. Add pork and stir-fry until thoroughly cooked, about 10 minutes. Add vegetables and sauce. Stir-fry just until vegetables are tender crisp.

STICKY DRUNK PIG ON A STICK

Needed on hand to complete this entrée: 10–12 (9-inch) skewers. Completely thaw entrée in the refrigerator. If using wooden skewers, soak them in water while meat is thawing. Thread pork pieces onto skewers. Prepare a medium-low fire in a gas or charcoal grill. Cook 15 to 18 minutes, turning occasionally and basting as desired. Do not baste during final 5 minutes of cooking. Discard remaining marinade.

GARLIC-STUDDED PORK LOIN

Completely thaw entrée in the refrigerator. Put roast and marinade in the slow cooker and cook on low for 8 to 10 hours.

ASIAN MARKET MARINADE FOR PORTOBELLO MUSHROOMS

Needed on hand to complete this entrée: 2 portobello mushroom caps. Completely thaw marinade in the refrigerator. Marinate mushroom caps for 1 hour. Prepare a medium-low fire in a gas or charcoal grill. Cook mushrooms 6 to 8 minutes per side, or until tender. Slice and serve over rice or noodles. Garnish with scallions, peanuts, or cilantro, if desired.

CAESAR PORTOBELLO MUSHROOMS

Needed on hand to complete this entrée: 2 portobello mushroom caps. Completely thaw marinade in the refrigerator. Marinate mushroom caps for 1 hour. Prepare a medium fire in a gas or charcoal grill. Cook mushrooms, turning occasionally, 10 to 12 minutes or until tender. Top each mushroom cap with 2 tablespoons Parmesan and grill until melted. *See main recipe for indoor cooking instructions.*

MAPLE PORTOBELLO MUSHROOMS

Needed on hand to complete this entrée: 2 portobello mushroom caps. Completely thaw marinade in the refrigerator. Marinate mushrooms for 1 hour. Prepare a medium fire in a gas or charcoal grill. Cook mushrooms, turning occasionally, 10 to 12 minutes or until tender. *See main recipe for indoor cooking instructions.*

FETA AND SPINACH LASAGNA ROLLS

Place lasagna rolls in a greased baking dish. Cover with foil; completely thaw in the refrigerator. Pour 2 cups marinara over rolls and top with 1 cup shredded mozzarella; replace foil. Bake at 350°F for 35 to 40 minutes, or until center is hot and cheese is melted.

ASPARAGUS AND POTATO OVEN FRITTATA

Completely thaw entrée in the refrigerator. Pour frittata into a lightly greased 8- × 8-inch baking dish. Bake at 425°F for 30 minutes, or until egg is cooked through and top is golden brown.

SPANAKOPITA

Thaw pastries in the refrigerator or bake straight from the freezer. Remove as many pastries as desired from the freezer. Remove plastic wrap. Place pastries on a greased baking sheet. Brush each pastry with 2 teaspoons melted butter. Bake at 400°F 17 to 19 minutes if frozen, 14 to 16 minutes if thawed.

RICE PILAF

Place frozen pilaf in a large saucepan and add 3 cups of water. Bring to a boil; reduce heat and cook, covered, for 20 minutes, or until water is completely absorbed.

THAI RED CURRY WITH VEGETABLES

Completely thaw one bag in the refrigerator. Pour sauce and vegetables into a medium saucepan; warm over medium heat. Serve as a side dish or as an entrée over steamed rice.

WILD RICE AND NUT BAKE

Completely thaw entrée in the refrigerator. Put the rice and nut mixture in a greased baking dish. Bake, uncovered, at 350°F for 1 to 1½ hours, or until set and a knife inserted into the center comes out clean.

SHRIMP CURRY

Completely thaw entrée in the refrigerator. In a large skillet over medium heat, bring the shrimp and curry sauce to a simmer. Do not boil. Serve over rice.

MANICOTTI

Thaw entrée in the refrigerator or bake it straight from the freezer. Remove plastic wrap and foil from baking dish and replace foil. Bake at 350°F for 45 minutes if thawed, 1 hour if frozen. Remove foil and continue baking until the noodles are tender.

VEGETABLE LASAGNA: LARGE PAN

Thaw entrée in the refrigerator or bake it straight from the freezer. Remove plastic wrap and foil from baking dish and replace foil. Place dish on a rimmed baking sheet and bake at 375°F for 1 hour if thawed, 1½ hours if frozen. Remove foil and continue baking until lasagna is bubbling and cheese is browned.

VEGETABLE LASAGNA: SMALL PAN

Thaw entrée in the refrigerator or bake it straight from the freezer. Remove plastic wrap and foil from baking dish and replace foil. Bake at 375°F for 45 minutes if thawed, 1 hour if frozen. Remove foil and continue baking until lasagna is bubbling and cheese is browned.

APPLES AND CHEDDAR

Completely thaw one side dish in the refrigerator. Put apple mixture in an ungreased baking dish and cover tightly with foil. Bake at 350°F for 45 minutes. Remove foil and continue baking until apples are soft and sauce is thick. Meanwhile, cook and stir pecan mixture over medium heat in a small skillet with 1 tablespoon water. After 5 minutes, or so, the sauce will caramelize. Remove from heat. Cool and crumble over baked apples.

BAKED POTATO CHOWDER
CREAM OF ASPARAGUS SOUP
CREAM OF MUSHROOM SOUP
TOMATO-BASIL SOUP

Completely thaw one bag in the refrigerator. Reheat soup in a large saucepan over medium-low heat. Do not boil.

SEAFOOD CREOLE

Completely thaw entrée in the refrigerator. Bring vegetable juice mixture to a boil in a large stockpot. Reduce heat and simmer for 20 minutes. Add seafood and continue simmering until seafood is thoroughly cooked, 5–7 minutes. Serve over rice.

GARLIC MASHED POTATOES

Thaw one side dish in the refrigerator or bake straight from the freezer. Remove plastic wrap and foil from baking dish and replace foil. Bake at 350°F for 1 hour if frozen, 30 minutes if thawed, or until potatoes are hot all the way through.

FRENCH ONION SOUP

Completely thaw entrée in the refrigerator. Place four ovenproof bowls on a rimmed baking sheet and divide onion mixture among them. Add 1 cup boiling water to each bowl. Top each soup with a slice of French bread. Divide the cheese evenly over the bread slices. Broil just until cheese melts and browns. Take care when serving the soup: the bowls will be very hot.

BLACK BEAN AND VEGETABLE CHILI

Completely thaw entrée in the refrigerator. Cook chili in a large saucepan over medium-low heat for 1 hour, or until liquid cooks off and chili is thick.

CHIPOTLE ROASTED-TOMATO SAUCE

Completely thaw one bag in the refrigerator. Use in a recipe calling for tomato sauce for a chipotle-enlivened dish, or simmer in a medium saucepan over medium-low heat for 5 to 10 minutes and pour over your favorite pasta.

BASIC RED SAUCE

Completely thaw one package in the refrigerator. Use as an ingredient in a recipe or simmer over low-medium heat for 20 minutes to serve over pasta.

WALNUT-PESTO BUTTER

Needed on hand to complete this entrée: 2 pounds salmon. Completely thaw one butter log in the refrigerator. Prepare a medium fire in a gas or charcoal grill. Cook salmon, turning occasionally, 10 to 15 minutes, or until fish flakes easily with a fork. Top with butter.

BROWN SUGAR AND BOURBON MARINADE FOR SALMON

Needed on hand to complete this entrée: 2 pounds salmon. Completely thaw marinade in the refrigerator. Place salmon in an ungreased 13- by 9-inch baking dish. Pour marinade over salmon and marinate 6 to 8 hours in the refrigerator. Prepare a medium fire in a gas or charcoal grill. Cook salmon, turning occasionally, 10 to 15 minutes or until fish flakes easily with a fork.

GORGONZOLA LEMON-PEPPER BUTTER

Completely thaw one butter log in the refrigerator. Toss with warm vegetables or pasta. Store in an airtight container in the refrigerator for up to 2 weeks or in the freezer for up to 1 month.

GORGONZOLA-PECAN BUTTER

Completely thaw one butter log in the refrigerator. Toss with warm vegetables or serve with rolls. Store in an airtight container in the refrigerator for up to 2 weeks or in the freezer for up to 1 month.

CHILI-LIME BUTTER FOR HALIBUT

Needed on hand to complete this entrée: 2 pounds halibut. Completely thaw one container of butter in the refrigerator. Grease a baking dish with some of the Chili-Lime Butter. Place halibut in the baking dish. Cover with the remaining butter compound and bake uncovered at 400°F for 20 minutes, or until fish is opaque and flakes easily with a fork.

BREAKFAST BURRITOS

Thaw the burritos in the refrigerator or reheat them straight from the freezer.
Microwave: Remove foil, defrost, and reheat.
Oven: Bake in foil at 375°F for 30 minutes if frozen, 300°F for 30 minutes if thawed.

GRANOLA

Place frozen granola on an ungreased baking sheet. Bake, stirring every 10 minutes, at 275°F for 30 minutes, or until golden brown. Cool and store in an airtight container.

CHEESE BISCUIT MIX

Completely thaw one batch in the refrigerator. Put the mixture in a medium bowl. Add ¾ cup milk and stir to form a dough. Turn dough out onto a lightly floured work surface and knead until dough holds together. Pat into a circle 2 inches thick. Cut into 8 wedges. Place wedges on an ungreased rimmed baking sheet. Bake at 425°F for 15 to 20 minutes, or until golden brown.

PUMPKIN MUFFINS

Thaw desired number of muffins in the refrigerator. Reheat in the microwave, in intervals of 10 to 15 seconds, until centers are warm.

CHEESE BITES

Thaw one bag in the refrigerator or bake straight from the freezer. Place cheese balls 3 inches apart on an ungreased baking sheet. Do not flatten. Bake at 425°F 15 to 17 minutes if frozen, 13 to 15 minutes if thawed.

STRAWBERRY SMOOTHIES

Thaw one bag in the refrigerator just enough to remove mix from bag. Put smoothie in a blender and add 1 cup cold water. Blend until smooth.
If starting with a thawed bag, blend with 1 cup ice in place of water.

TROPICAL FRUIT SMOOTHIES

Thaw one bag in the refrigerator just enough to remove mix from bag. Put smoothie in a blender and add 1 cup cold water. Blend until smooth.

If starting with a thawed bag, blend with 1 cup ice in place of water.

GINGER COOKIES

Thaw one bag in the refrigerator or bake straight from the freezer. Place cookies 3 inches apart on an ungreased baking sheet. Do not use parchment paper; do not flatten. Bake at 350°F 15 to 17 minutes if frozen, 12 to 14 minutes if thawed. Cool on baking sheet for 2 minutes; transfer to a cooling rack.

FIVE-SPICE COOKIES

Place frozen cookies 3 inches apart on a parchment-lined baking sheet. Bake at 375°F for 8 to 10 minutes, or until tops crack. Cool on baking sheet for 2 minutes; transfer to a cooling rack.

LEMON-LAVENDER BUTTER COOKIES

Place frozen cookies 3 inches apart on a parchment-lined baking sheet Bake at 375°F for 8 to 10 minutes, or until tops crack. Cool on baking sheet for 2 minutes; transfer to a cooling rack.

OATMEAL COOKIES WITH COCONUT AND MANGO

Completely thaw one bag in the refrigerator. Place cookies 3 inches apart on a parchment-lined baking sheet. Flatten slightly with a fork. Bake at 350°F for 14 to 16 minutes. Cool on baking sheet for 2 minutes; transfer to a cooling rack.

VERY VANILLA SNICKERDOODLES

Place frozen cookies 3 inches apart on a parchment-lined baking sheet. Bake at 375°F for 8 to 10 minutes, or until tops crack. Cool on baking sheet for 2 minutes; transfer to a cooling rack.

METRIC CONVERSION CHARTS

Unless you have finely calibrated measuring equipment, conversions between U.S. and metric measurements will be somewhat inexact. It's important to convert the measurements for all of the ingredients in a recipe to maintain the same proportions as the original.

WEIGHT		
To convert	**to**	**multiply**
ounces	grams	ounces by 28.35
pounds	grams	pounds by 453.5
pounds	kilograms	pounds by 0.45

VOLUME		
To convert	**to**	**multiply**
teaspoons	milliliters	teaspoons by 4.93
tablespoons	milliliters	tablespoons by 14.79
fluid ounces	milliliters	fluid ounces by 29.57
cups	milliliters	cups by 236.59
cups	liters	cups by 0.24
pints	milliliters	pints by 473.18
pints	liters	pints by 0.473
quarts	milliliters	quarts by 946.36
quarts	liters	quarts by 0.946
gallons	liters	gallons by 3.785

TEMPERATURE		
To convert	**to**	
Fahrenheit	Celsius	subtract 32 from Fahrenheit temperature, multiply by 5, then divide by 9

RESOURCE LIST

MAGAZINES

COOKS ILLUSTRATED

www.cooksillustrated.com

A bimonthly publication with recipes, kitchen tips, and product reviews from the consumer's perspective.

COMPANIES

BOB'S RED MILL NATURAL FOODS

800-349-2173

www.bobsredmill.com

Offers naturally milled flours, grains, gluten-free products for sale, and free recipes on their website. Their whole grain store, cooking classes, and kitchen are open to the public.

PENZEYS SPICES

800-741-7787

www.penzeys.com

Offers spices, extracts, and assorted gift packs for sale by mail order or online.

BOOKS

Balmuth, Deborah, ed. *Herb Mixtures and Spicy Blends.* Storey Publishing, 1996. Offers many recipes for spice blends. Individuals watching their sodium intake will appreciate the chapter on salt-free blends.

Costenbader, Carol. *The Big Book of Preserving the Harvest.* Storey Publishing, 2002. Recipes and instruction on preserving fruits, vegetables, and herbs. Includes time charts for blanching and freezing.

Eliason, Karine, Nevada Harward, and Madeline Westover. *Make-a-Mix.* Running Press, 2007. Gives a good selection of economical pantry and seasoning mix recipes.

Logan, Karen. *Clean House, Clean Planet.* Pocket Books, 1997. Recipes for nontoxic home-cleaning supplies. Offers price comparisons between home-mixed cleaners and commercial brands, so you can see how much money you save by making your own.

Marcin, Marietta Marshall. *Herbal Tea Gardens.* Storey Publishing, 1999. Features many recipes for hand mixing your own teas from garden herbs.

Sahni, Julie. *Savoring Spices and Herbs.* William Morrow & Co., 1996. A good resource for unique rubs and seasoning blends.

Siegel-Maier, Karen. *The Naturally Clean Home.* Storey Publishing, 1999. More recipes and tips for cleaning your home without toxic commercial cleaners.

Topp, Ellie, and Margaret Howard. *The Complete Book of Year-Round Small Batch Preserving.* Firefly Books, 2001. Recipes and instruction on preserving small quantities of fruits, vegetables, oils, and vinegars.

ACKNOWLEDGMENTS

We are grateful to be surrounded by wonderful people, both professionally and personally, who have contributed to our project. Before this book ever made it to this incarnation, it had another life as a small self-published volume. Shawnee Halligan was an original contributor. Her sunny disposition and positive outlook made her a delight to work with.

Then, as now, we are privileged to work with many talented people who contribute their amazing skills and vision to this product behind the scenes through design, layout, editing, food photography, and printing. We appreciate the opportunity to work with Storey Publishing. We never knew the process could be so pleasant.

Thank you to our recipe testers. We are grateful that you were willing to undertake the task of trying new recipes, wading through our notes and doing exactly as you were told!

We acknowledge the food enthusiasts, recipe writers, and culinary experts at large from whom we have gleaned ideas, tips, and much inspiration. Because of the work others have done, we have been able to build on the foundation set before us.

Loyal customers, old and new, we thank you for your enthusiasm and warm feedback. It has been encouraging.

KATI

Carl Jung once said, "The shoe that fits one person pinches another; there is no recipe for living that suits all cases." I am eternally grateful to my husband, parents, children, in-laws, family, and friends for their support while working on this book. Without you all I would not have had the audacity and courage to create my own "recipe."

LINDSAY

Many years ago someone, I know not who, bought me a brand new chest freezer and had it delivered to my home anonymously. I was stunned by and overjoyed with the gift. Over the years, I have often thought of the generous secret donor and wished I could give my thanks. In many ways, that gift was the beginning of the journey that led me here.

That unexpected gift also represents the way I feel about the precious people who envelop me in my life. My circle of loved ones is faceless to those who read this book, as the anonymous freezer donor is to me, But it cannot go unsaid that without the blessings they've bestowed upon me, I would not have accomplished anything. To those who have unfailingly believed in, supported, and encouraged this project — my husband, children, parents, siblings, in-laws, aunts and uncles, and friends — may I be a blessing to you in return.

INDEX

Page references in *italics* indicate recipe freezer labels.